SLOT SMARTS

SLOT SMARTS

WINNING STRATEGIES
AT THE
SLOT MACHINE

CLAUDE HALCOMBE

A LYLE STUART BOOK
Published by Carol Publishing Group

Carol Publishing Group Edition, 1997

A Lyle Stuart Book
Published by Carol Publishing Group
Lyle Stuart is a registered trademark of Carol Communications, Inc.

Editorial, sales and distribution, rights and permissions inquiries
should be addressed to Carol Publishing Group, 120 Enterprise Avenue,
Secaucus, N.J. 07094

In Canada: Canadian Manda Group, One Atlantic Avenue, Suite 105,
Toronto, Ontario M6K 3E7

Carol Publishing Group books may be purchased in bulk at special
discounts for sales promotions, fund-raising, or educational purposes.
Special editions can be created to specifications. For details, contact
Special Sales Department, Carol Publishing Group, 120 Enterprise Avenue,
Secaucus, N.J. 07094

Manufactured in the United States of America
10 9 8 7 6 5 4 3

Library of Congress Cataloging-in-Publication Data

Halcombe, Claude.
    Slot smarts : winning strategies at the slot machine / Claude
Halcombe.
        p.   cm.
    "A Lyle Stuart book."
    ISBN 0-8184-0584-8 (pbk.)
    1. Slot machines. 2. Gambling. I Title.
GV1311.S56H35   1996
688.7'52—dc20   96-25071
                                                          CIP

America's new growth entertainment industry is sending multi-media messages.

The messages are strong, loud, persistent, and the calls are designed to reach every one of us...

Contents

Preface: The Working Man

A few years ago I met a man who said he was working. Since we were in a casino at five in the morning, and there were slot machines north, south, east and west of us, his claim seemed ridiculous. "Working? Who's he kidding?" I thought to myself.

I was no gambler. We had stopped overnight in Las Vegas to see the sights, and, unable to sleep, I had ventured downstairs to the casino where I tried my luck with a few slots and lost a few dollars before I chanced upon the only person in the slot machine area who knew precisely why he was there and what he was doing.

He was young, maybe in his late twenties, early thirties, distinguished neither in attire nor appearance. I had passed him several times already that morning without noticing anything about him in particular; just another faceless, nameless man...woman...body...pulling at the levers on a sequence of slot machines.

Our meeting came about this way: I had done my $10 on one machine and was wandering around looking for a likely place to win or lose the next $10. At the end of a carousel in the middle of the casino, I encountered two men watching another at a dollar machine a little further down the line.

I heard one of them say, "That's his third lot of sevens in the last ten minutes," and the other guy replied, "Been doing that all night. He must be thousands up by now."

"But what's he losing between wins?" I ventured dubiously, noting to myself that, for a so-called big winner, the player didn't seem to have many dollar slugs around. From where I stood, I couldn't see any in the machine tray and the $100 slide beside his glass of coffee was only half full. Where was all the money if he was breaking the bank?

"He keeps his winnings in the machine then cashes out every now and again," one of the men told me. "I've seen him cash out half a dozen times tonight. Goes away with four, five racks, comes back with one, and starts over."

"At the same machine?"

"No, at another machine but he seems to be keeping to the same group. Third time I've seen him on that one. A while ago he was on the other side where he had been about an hour before. Won big both times there, too."

"How can you be so sure he's winning every time?"

The speaker didn't seem to like my question. He retorted, "Well, if a guy arrives with a $100 slide and goes away with $300 or $400, that's sure like winning to me."

I acknowledged he had a point but further revealed my ignorance of slot machines by adding, "He must be tapping the credits in the machine when he runs out."

"One hundred dollars in, $300 or $400 out. You don't need to be any rocket scientist to work that one out," he said very curtly.

My interest piqued, I decided to investigate for myself and sat down two machines away from the man at a slot which looked much the same as the one he was playing. As I did so, mixed sevens came up for him again.

"You seem to be having terrific luck this morning," I said. "Didn't I see you do that a while back?"

He glanced my way, paused a moment as though reluctant to answer, then made what seemed a bizarre, almost arrogant, statement, "You can call it luck. I call it inevitable." And he went back to watching the meter on his machine.

Intrigued, I watched the tally counter, too. When it stopped adding the new win, the reading (which I soon learned was the accumulating total) was more than $800.

"Well, you seem to be doing all right now but that can't last," I ventured again. "You can't control the machine."

He shot me a piercing look, "No, but I can control me," he said, "And that's more than half the battle."

A cocktail waitress came around offering drinks, and he asked for another black coffee. They seemed well acquainted, so I followed her and said, "That guy seems to be on a lucky streak. What's in the coffee you're giving him?"

"Oh him," she laughed. "He's on a lucky streak most nights. I can tell you one thing for sure, it has nothing to do with the coffee."

"He's a regular then?"

"Regular? Just about lives in the place. Has for months. Plays four, five days a week, most every week, and always those same machines."

"Lucky him!" I exclaimed. "He must be rich. Only a rich man could afford to play every day."

"Well, he mightn't have been rich before but he likely is by now," she observed. "He's about the only guy I know who seems to leave this place winning just about every day."

"So he tells you," I said. "How do you really know?"

"I have eyes. Other people get a win now and again but most everybody in a casino finishes up losing. That guy's got an edge somehow. It works for me, too. He tips well."

I resolved then and there to learn more about this man who was winning so often even the waitress noticed.

I decided on a direct approach. I would ask him outright. Maybe he would give away some secrets. I sat down beside him again and said, "Well, if this isn't luck, is there a formula?"

Looking me over carefully before speaking, he ventured, "Not much I can tell you." He paused again. "You have to work at it like anything else, and work hard. This is no game."

There was that word *work*.

I recall now that our conversation was rather one-sided, a lot of prompting from me, not much of a response from him. I quickly decided that this man was not the boastful type; he seemed taciturn, reluctant to give out too much detail about what he was doing.

Somehow, though, over the next ten or fifteen minutes I managed to get him to open up a little and talk to me. In those precious few minutes, my education began.

I did not count the number of times the word *work* came up during our discussion. My best recollection is he used it in a variety of contexts at least a dozen times, almost as though he felt a compulsion to come back to the word and reinforce the message that work was the cornerstone of his slot machine philosophy.

His comments: "I work five days a week, same as other people." "I don't take this lightly; this is work." "I work to win." I had no doubt he meant every word. This man was indeed hard at work, working at the task of winning.

And working successfully—if there was any truth in what he told me of his record over the past few months. My subsequent slot machine experiences indicate there was. However, since I cannot vouch for the accuracy of his claims or the amount of his winnings, I will not risk misleading you with what I deduced as his strategy.

I am not naive. I realize most people are prone to exaggerate their wins and minimize their losses in the retelling. "Gambler's hype," I've heard it called. But then this man was quite different from my image of a gambler. In his approach to the task at hand, he seemed thoroughly professional.

Perhaps it was a lucky coincidence, an accident, or an omen of things to come, but I decided to apply some of my new acquaintance's routine after he cashed out and was gone again with an armful of dollar slides. Perhaps some of his luck would rub off on me.

Since I knew nothing at that time about differences in slot

machines, I elected to stick with those I had seen him working and hope I could apply some of his techniques.

Lo and behold, I turned my earlier losses into two winning sessions that returned a welcome profit for my efforts.

To me, this slot machine phenomenon seemed an opportunity to check something out and, in so doing, find out a little more about my own strengths and weaknesses. Could I apply the disciplines the man claimed were essential to short- or long-term success?

After several weeks of deliberation, I decided to allocate funds and conduct tests for myself.

I realized, of course, that I knew virtually nothing about this man or his actual methods. After all, there was no way I could have learned a fraction of what I would need to know from a short conversation in a casino with a stranger who may or may not have been everything he claimed. I had to admit the whole scenario seemed improbable.

Nonetheless, my gut feeling was that I'd found a man who indeed knew what he had to do to beat the slot machines consistently. He was working and he was winning.

Could I do that too? The question was intriguing.

Six years and many wins later, I have the answer.

Acknowledgments

About two years after making the decision to test my theories and luck on slots, I began to think seriously about writing a book.

As I went about gathering information I thought essential for realistic prospects of withstanding one-armed bandit assaults on the pocketbook, I became aware of the need for a sensible guide to help Mr. and Ms. Everyman. Discreetly watching people in casinos day after day, venturing a few questions when the opportunity arose, I began to realize most slot players were like myself when I started out, untutored and ill-informed; unwitting conspirators in the exercise of losing regularly.

In resort cities, even the locals who play slots frequently seemed to have scant knowledge of the modern slot machine and were apparently oblivious to the contribution their own behavior was making to their escalating losses.

I recall an early-morning regular. Her blackened glove was a sure indication that she spent lots of time at this hobby. She seemed to do fairly well and most mornings would quit when ahead. The lady held dominion over a group of slots, putting holds on her favored machines when she was off playing others. On days when she was not faring so well, some trigger would send her home before much damage had been done. She was the exception. Even among the gloved set, few have a game plan. Emotions, mood, and luck seem to dictate the patterns of play and most times the majority linger on long enough to turn their winnings moments sour.

So if the experienced don't, won't, or can't control their behavior and their fortunes, what is the chance occasional players can keep money in pocket? I hunted out books on slots. There weren't many and, as I soon discovered, precious few of value.

I could not have written this book without the help and expertise of many others.

As I learned early to concentrate my activities in certain casinos, it follows I first turned to executives in those establishments. Among those who cheerfully responded to my questions and granted me the favor of their valuable time and access to their facilities, I especially thank Ron Johnson, Vice President of Gaming Operations at the Riviera, and Hans Dorweiler, General Manager at the Westward Ho. The staff at both casinos have also been most cooperative.

Jennifer Burgess and Stephen Brewster of The Promus Companies provided field surveys, made research material available to me, and relayed my queries to several of their casinos including Harrah's Las Vegas where Slots Manager, Michael Gausling, recovering from a ski accident, completed a comprehensive questionnaire. However, the legal eagles in Memphis may have decided my questions touched sensitive areas. The questionnaire was not returned to me.

The slots staff at Palace Station and Vegas World (now The Stratosphere) were helpful but management at both casinos ignored my questionnaires and several requests for personal interviews.

I had much better luck with the regulators. Kevin O'Toole, attorney for the New Jersey Gaming Enforcement Commission, answered my queries readily. In Nevada, Harlan Elges and his staff at the Gaming Control Board were friendly and helpful. I especially acknowledge the assistance given me at various times by Joan Hammack, Chuck Anderson and Todd Westergard.

The Las Vegas Convention and Visitor Authority has furnished me with its comprehensive Visitor Profile Studies in each of the past four years and Justin Jackson in the Research department has readily and promptly responded to my frequent phone questions during that time.

I very much appreciate the help of my editors at Carol Publishing Group, Allan Wilson and Colette Russen.

My thanks to the hundreds of nameless people, regulars and occasional players alike, who stimulated my curiousity and set me to the task of bringing some measure of balance to the equation of winning and losing.

Introduction

I consider my chance meeting with the successful slot machine worker fortuitous, a watershed encounter that inspired me to action in a field in which I had no previous interest. It has had an indelible impact on me.

I was no gambler then. Paradoxical as it may seem, I do not consider myself a gambler now. I don't have the stomach for gambling. The thought of losing a wallet of hard-earned cash in a few minutes of painful, relentless extraction makes me cringe. I am not a good loser.

I say I am not a gambler, yet I go to Las Vegas regularly. That city has become my destination of choice, the casinos a domain where I feel comfortable. I bankroll several trips to Las Vegas and the slot machines each year. I win 70 percent to 80 percent of the time. Only once have I lost three days in a row, and most days my winnings exceed my worst-day losses.

Like that working man, I am under no illusions. The old one-armed bandit tag is well deserved. Slot machines are pirates. They can relieve you of more money in a short time than almost any other gambling pursuit.

Slot machines don't have favorites. They are indifferent to your occupation or social standing and are contemptuous of the systems or tricks you may bring into play in your efforts to beat them.

They feed you a few dollars here, a few dollars there, then swallow it back in big gulps, rapidly consuming your stake, your winnings, and your available credit if you let them.

Slot machines, and by extension casino owners, don't care how you came by your money or whether you can afford to gamble; they treat doctors, lawyers, beggarmen, and thieves the same way—they cheerfully gobble up whatever money you feed them.

Yet, knowing all this and being fully cognizant of the risks, I now go to Las Vegas and on most trips I win. What is my secret?

I win because I manage my luck better than most. (Remember the term Managed Luck. I will refer to it repeatedly.

I win because I know the odds are always against me and I must have a winning game plan.

I win because I concentrate on slots with which I am familiar.

I win because I have developed a strategy for leaving a slot machine with most of the money I have won.

I win because I have a fixed daily stake I will not exceed.

I win because I do not go from casino to casino until I strike it lucky.

I win because I limit my number of casino visits and am selective about the casinos I frequent.

I win because I plan my time and work my plan better than most other players.

I have taken the lessons I learned from that chance encounter and developed my own strategies. I work those strategies always—come hell or high water.

Since I met that working man, I have paid taxes on my gambling winnings each year. Some years are better than others but each has been profitable. Nobody can claim to have a successful slots strategy on the basis of a few lucky wins, no matter how big they may be. Consistency is the true test of success. Can you win more often than you lose? Can you win more money on your good days than you lose on your bad days? Can you get ahead and stay ahead?

I already know I will have winnings to declare again this year even though I have made only two trips to Las Vegas thus far, and don't expect to win any jackpots. I can be so certain of success because I will manage my luck. I have programmed myself to work and win, and work and win I will.

I cannot guarantee that using my methods you will win a million dollars or even $50,000. In fact, I can almost guarantee you will not hit any huge jackpots. I cannot guarantee you will finish $10,000 or even $1,000 ahead over two, three, five, or ten casino visits.

I do guarantee you *can* and *will* win more and lose less when you embrace the philosophy and slot machine practices I share in this book.

SLOT SMARTS

1

Objectives of This Book

This book provides basic information and guidelines.

It is not my intention to endorse slot machine activities by encouraging readers to scan this package then charge out and risk their fortunes on one-armed bandits. At the same time, I don't wish to discourage those who already patronize the casinos or dissuade others from taking their chances.

I cannot recommend you pursue gambling in any form— lotteries, horse races, poker, slot machines, keno, the office pool, whatever. I know nothing about you, your pysche or personal proclivities, your finances, your family, your capacity to absorb details and act on information, your sense of personal and civic responsibility, or your personal goals.

Slot machines are not for everybody, and I do not know whether they are good or bad for you. I am not prepared to venture that kind of judgment.

What I will do is tell you about the personal discipline and temperament essential for success with slot machines.

This information could help you determine whether slot machines have a place in your life. For many, they do not. You alone can make that decision. I trust my profiles will help.

I will also indicate how much free money you should have available before you visit a casino and whether you should play nickel, quarter, or dollar machines. I will stress the importance of ensuring you do not divert money from any of your other personal or family obligations.

All in all, I am prepared to give you the benefit of my research and experience in devising strategies which have worked satisfactorily for me in the business of making money from slot machines.

I will make no exaggerated claims which cannot be substantiated. I am not a million dollar winner but I am a regular winner. Again, for our purposes, that is more important than advocating false philosophies based solely on one lucky jackpot win in Megabucks, Nevada Nickels, or Quartermania.

Warning: Though I think I have several winning slots strategies, I am not persuaded I could make a living from this hobby.

I believe I would have a better chance than most people; in fact, I have little doubt I could derive *some* level of income from slot machines. But for now my profitable hobby will remain just that, a hobby, not an occupation.

I do not subscribe to the theory that small successes will automatically become big successes given more exposure. I know the reverse is more likely to hold true where slots are involved.

Later in this book we will talk about what I call Windows of Opportunity. Along with Managed Luck, these windows are critical even to short-term success, but I have found it is virtually impossible to expand or add windows to the house of good fortune, which is what I would be trying to do were I to attempt to make my living from slots.

This is my protection. I enjoy several casino visits each year, but I have no desire to spend more time in them.

There are many wonderful activities in life we should find time to experience and enjoy. Perspective is important. I can find all the fun, pleasure, and enjoyment I need from making four, five, or sometimes six short trips to Las Vegas and the slot machines each year.

And I not only have fun when I go, I make money.

This book serves a dual function. The early sections provide an information base. (Casinos could provide similar guidelines for their patrons—a P.R. natural.)

This foundation is vital. You should know the facts and be in a position to reconcile the realities with your personal situation or idiosyncrasies before you decide whether or not to play slot machines.

The center of the book is devoted to:

- elementary preparations such as defining goals compatible with your finances
- choosing a casino with an environment where you feel comfortable
- recognizing which slot machines to play and which to avoid

In other words, this section covers enhancing your winning prospects and positioning yourself to maintain better control.

We then move to the fundamentals of winning, the keys to success, and overall strategies. Finally, I will introduce four work plans. Each has a function slightly different from the others and will appeal to a specific category of reader. All four share common purposes—to make casino visits more fun and to turn occasional and perennial losers alike into more frequent winners.

There is a danger here. Don't skip the front information sections and go straight to the strategies at the back of the book. You will do yourself no favors by taking a shortcut.

If you jump ahead, you will deprive yourself of the value of the whole presentation, and I doubt you will achieve the financial and other benefits which could be yours if you follow the sequence of material.

The sequence and design of this book are no accident. I expect many readers will want to keep it as a handy reference and thumb through it as they would a tour guide.

Reinforcement of knowledge and technique is important. It is no easy task to position yourself to win consistently on slots. Your prospects of staying with any work-to-win discipline will improve significantly given the right tools.

For that reason, the book is a quick and easy reference and each work plan has an introductory summary which highlights key elements.

For what it is worth, I would not venture into any casino without a reference card to keep me focused and on the right track. Because I have been doing this for several years and know most of the pitfalls, I may refer to the card only once or twice on a trip. Yet I know I want it with me. It is an essential part of my preparation and discipline.

I have also included a page from the daily activity record I use to keep an accurate tally of my activities. Don't underestimate the importance of keeping such a diary. I am convinced it is imperative that you know where you stand financially at all stages of your slot machine sessions.

Not only should you know whether you are winning or losing, you should recognize which slots are generating your wins and which are cutting into your profits.

There is another important function for the daily activity record. Gambling winnings are taxable. By winnings, I mean the total of all winnings after adjusting for losses, not just any wins you have over the $1,200 threshold which will generate a tax form and casino report to the Internal Revenue Service.

I strongly advocate absolute honesty in reporting your slot machine profits. Without a detailed record, you will be hard put to compile the information you need in a successful year. The diary is not only your personal record, it can document your wins and losses for the IRS.

I hope you enjoy this book. More important, I trust you will win and win often when you look for fun or go for the gold on the slot machines.

2

Why Is Your
Money Wet?

The first time I won a jackpot was at the Riviera in Las Vegas. The sequence of events seems laughable in retrospect but was not so amusing at the time. Nonetheless, the episode illustrates several facets of human behavior in the casino environment and is worth recounting.

My last slots session was due to end two hours before I left for the airport. My bags were packed and I had already checked out of my room. All I had to do when I finished the final session was retrieve my luggage from the porter and catch the shuttle bus at the casino door.

From experience before and since, I am always rather cautious about last-day slot activity. This can be a dangerous period in any trip, especially if the overall financial results have been less rosy than expected.

It is more difficult to stay with the game plan when there are losses to recover or you are looking for that elusive worthwhile payout to crown the trip. This is the time when you can get reckless, sometimes desperate.

Sir Henry Newbolt's poem on the game of cricket, "Vitaï Lampada," opens:

There's a breathless hush in the close tonight—
Ten to make and the match to win—
A bumping pitch and a blinding light,
An hour to play and the last man in...

If you can sense the tension in Sir Henry's words even though you know little about cricket, you will better appreciate the pressures besieging slot machine players down to the last hour, maybe the last $10, and victory still to be won.

The pressure is particularly intense for those who find the discipline of sticking to a game plan difficult to maintain any time let alone when the clock is running headlong toward departure. We are all keen to make things happen somehow and go for broke...which too often is how we will finish if we yield to these urges.

On this day I was about 20 percent up on my daily stake and expected to be off to the airport with a fair profit.

My session at the previous slot was a wash, and when I moved to the next machine, I started along what I consider an average activity curve—small returns more or less in line with the payout frequency I would expect from that type slot, an IGT Red, White, and Blue three coiner.

I was about halfway into the session and coming off two small wins in five or six spins when the top line came up with all coins in. It is a great feeling when you realize the sevens are in the right color sequence and all pay lines are going for you.

In other words, you have just won the ten thousand coin jackpot.

The flashing lights heralding a jackpot win, combined with the din as the payout started to rattle through the first six hundred coins (the maximum number that machine pays without an attendant), brought people from all directions.

I was quickly surrounded by an army of enthusiastic spectators vying for a chance to slap me on the back, to shake my hand or touch my shoulder—or the machine—to bring them luck.

Casino officials took a lot longer to get there. When the floorman finally arrived and checked the pay line and pay board to confirm the amount I had won, he made a simple mistake. He misread the order of the red, white, and blue sevens and saw them as mixed sevens, an error anybody could make with all three colors on the pay line.

The machine payout had stopped at around 210 coins. It had either jammed or was low in money; nothing unusual, this happens frequently. The redcoat announced that the casino owed me another thirty coins to bring the payout up to 240 coins for mixed sevens with three coins in.

I quickly corrected him. He acknowledged his mistake immediately but the damage was done. Forever suspicious of casino ethics, several in the crowd started to mutter, characterizing this incident as a blatant attempt on the part of casino management to hoodwink me out of my winnings.

One man leaned over and whispered in my ear something to the effect, "I know these casino operators. You're lucky you know what you are doing and are ready for them. Otherwise they'd have done you in just like they did a friend of mine when he thought he had won a jackpot." He proceeded to tell me some story which did not make sense. I stopped listening.

Two points here. The first is trust or, rather, the pervasive lack of it. It seems to be a quirk of our culture, viewing casinos as several shades the other side of crooked.

I don't know where this perception comes from. Perhaps it arises from the persistent media infatuation with the organized crime connections of some of the older gambling establishments on the Strip, a bad scene thirty years or more behind us. Or perhaps it is related somehow to the opposition of religious organizations which preach that gambling is sinful.

Whatever the cause, gaming establishments are not held in

high public regard even today when the operating climate is so different from days gone by.

This is unfortunate and unfair. Casinos are big business enterprises, mostly public companies, and all subject to the intense scrutiny of the various state gaming authorities.

Were they to attempt anything nefarious, they would likely be exposed and punished more quickly and more severely than almost any other type of business because of the tighter enforcement environment and, in some jurisdictions, the presence of regulatory agents on the premises to ensure laws are followed to the letter. Even minor technical transgressions can bring prompt, sometimes disproportionate, punitive actions. Casinos have been closed for little more than failing to follow the mandated record-keeping procedures.

The fallout from this attitude among the general public is that many of us miss the chance to enjoy casinos and win fair and square simply because our minds have been addled by preconceived notions.

An astonishing number of people have told me in all seriousness that casinos adjust hot machines, that somewhere up above the slot machine floor lurk bands of unsavory characters charged with the responsibility of turning off the machines just before they strike big.

I guess in the old days we would have said these evil people carry huge magnets to distort the spinning system on the slots. Now, in the age of computers, I hear they spend their time reprogramming the machines to ensure they will never pay out those big wins.

We hurt only ourselves with these simplistic ideas. There is enough caprice in the modern computerized slot machine to make winning difficult enough without resorting to dirty tricks. After all, the odds always favor the house and the casino win is already guaranteed by the retention percentage in the slot programs; in fact, it is about the only thing guaranteed in the whole establishment.

Rather than blame the casinos for our lack of success, we should concentrate on what we can do to change our fortunes. And there is a lot, as I will attempt to show you. For now, I strongly recommend you rid yourself of any misconception that the dice are loaded. There are no dice in slots.

The second point concerns identification. After we corrected the error in the amount of payout due, I was asked for photo I.D. Because of a chronic problem which affects my head movement, I do not have a driver's license and so had no photo I.D. in my wallet. Credit cards, business cards, health insurance cards would not suffice. The Riviera insisted on photo I.D. and would not accept even its own slot club card despite the fact that when it was issued I had produced sufficient documentation to establish I was the person I claimed to be.

Eventually we overcame that problem when I convinced one of the higher ups that he could phone the toll-free number on my Medic Alert bracelet to verify my identity. He took my word for it and paid me. I caught my plane only because departure was delayed over half an hour.

As soon as I arrived home, I made arrangements for a state identification card, complete with photograph. I wasn't about to go through that again.

Since then, I have noticed most casinos ask for photo I.D. for virtually everything—at check in, entering a tournament, opening a keno account. My recommendation is be sure you have yours with you before you enter the casino. It is a vital part of your winning inventory. I hope you will have a big money occasion to use it.

Which brings us to the strange title of this chapter, "Why Is Your Money Wet?"

When I went to the change booth, the attendant ran into difficulties. The coin counter kept jamming and she was quickly losing patience.

Suddenly she turned to me and asked, "Why is your money wet? You're ruining my machine."

"How would I know?" I responded, which did little to placate her. Innocence (or ignorance) was no defense.

"Next time, go to some other change booth. I'm not having the likes of you mess up my equipment," she muttered.

Bewildered, I turned for explanation to the redcoat who had accompanied me to the booth. He smiled at my question. "People order beer and the glasses get tipped over in the coin tray," he told me. "They seem more interested in the beer than in the slots. The coins get sticky and choke the coin counter."

If I didn't already avoid alcohol during my sessions, I think I would have made that decision on the spot. I enjoy a beer as much as the next person but I drink only fruit juice or coffee when I am working the machines. I save the beer or whiskey for a celebration toast after a big win.

3

Huge Pool but Slim Pickings

A short time ago I read an article in a small newspaper in Texas. What caught my eye was an aphorism attributed to an old eccentric the journalist knew as a child, "If you don't believe there's gold buried in your backyard, there ain't no sense in digging."

Well there is a lot of gold being buried every day in the slot machine yards of casinos all over the country, but although those yards are getting bigger and closer to home, for most of us, the digging ain't easy.

I have said before that slot machines are great gobblers of money. I have also heard only a turkey would play them. Well, there must be plenty of turkeys out there.

Whatever we choose to say about them, the reality is that as a nation we risk more money on one-armed bandits than on any other form of regulated gambling, including horse races.

In Nevada, the statewide casino income from coin-operated devices in the 189 establishments with annual revenues of more than $1 million exceeded $3.685 billion in 1993, an incredible 62.7 percent of total gaming revenues.

Now get this folks! The average slots hold in those locations hovers around 4.7 percent; so, in 1993, a stratospheric $78.5 billion must have gone through slots, keno, and video poker machines.

That is one heap of money, and remember, the figure refers to a single state and does not include slot operator circuits.

Despite the efforts of groups opposed to gambling, each year the popularity of casinos soars, and the amount of money wagered on slot machines rockets ever higher.

Between 1993 and 1995, the number of visitors to Las Vegas increased almost 5.5 million to more than 29 million, a 23.3 percent increase. In the same period, gross gaming revenues (or the casino hold) in Clark County alone, climbed from $4.727 billion to $5.717 billion, an increase of 21 percent.

Nationwide, casino revenues have more than doubled in the past five years and those ubiquitous, coin-operated devices continue to dominate the activity, accounting for around two-thirds of every dollar spent on gaming and virtually all casino profits. Is it then any wonder slot machines take up most of the floor space in every casino?

An article in a March, 1994, issue of *U.S. News and World Report* predicted that in 1995 gamblers could lose as much as $35 billion nationwide, much of it in casinos. (Industry estimates put the actual 1995 casino win at $20.3 billion).

Slots and video poker machines will continue to dominate the gaming scene. Indications are that their share, as a percentage of the total casino win, will continue to surge each year into the foreseeable future. By the turn of the century, players could be leaving more than $22 billion in the swollen bellies of coin devices across the country.

Talk about gorging!

In 1988, only two states had licensed casinos. That number has now increased to twenty-six and will reach at least twenty-eight by 1997. One recent survey predicts there will be riverboat casinos in nineteen states by the year 2002.

In addition to this expansion in the United States, there are now casinos or similar establishments in virtually every province in Canada, thus completing a North American conversion to blanket acceptance of casinos and gambling, a phenomenon which has taken place in the space of only eight years.

As with revenues, the number of people patronizing casinos has more than doubled since 1990 and people are going more frequently. By 1993, casino visits were already dwarfing attendance at baseball games. Within five years, we are likely to find casinos draw more people than professional and intercollegiate sports combined.

Not only are new states venturing into the gaming business, there are more locations within each state and at the traditional meccas.

There seems no end in sight to the boom times in Las Vegas. Three colossal new hotel-casinos and a number of smaller establishments have opened there in the past two years, pushing total hotel rooms above the ninety thousand mark. Despite the competition most of the older, established places are setting revenue records each year. Average city-wide occupancy rates are now running at 89 percent on an annual basis and an incredible 94 percent at weekends. Compare this with the 81 percent room occupancy in 1986.

And the building doesn't stop. Vegas World, which I'll mention again later, has become the newly-opened Stratosphere, a 2,500 room, $315 million complex that towers over the downtown end of the Strip. New York, New York will open its 2,150 room recreation of the New York skyline in early 1997 not too far from the Bellagio, the $1 billion, 3,000 room venture from the owners of the Mirage. In between, the similarly sized Monte Carlo will have opened its doors to the public before this book reaches the market. Both the Luxor and Harrah's will add several hundred rooms in 1997–98.

On the Nevada-California border, a family entertainment

complex called Buffalo Bill's opened in late 1994. In addition to 600 rooms and the inevitable walls of slot machines and table games for adults, this omnibus enterprise features what owners claim is the world's tallest roller coaster, a water log ride, a western ghost town, movie theatre, and a 6,500 seat sports arena.

Of the twenty-nine-million two-hundred-thousand visitors to Las Vegas last year, 28 percent or more than eight million were on their first visit to the city. Strangely, only 6 percent of all visitors specified gambling as the principal reason for making their trips, which suggest that despite the wider acceptance of casino gambling as entertainment, many of us are reluctant to admit we gamble. We would prefer to say we are "on vacation" as two-thirds of visitors said in response to a 1995 survey.

Conversely, 89 percent of visitors admitted they themselves gambled at least once during their stay and 52 percent tried their luck on the slot machines. A whopping 64 percent concentrated their activities on quarter slots.

A closer study of the statistics indicates that while more than half the visitors budgeted $100 or less per day for gambling, the typical visitor risked $514 during a three night–four day visit and gambled more than four hours per day... a lot of money and time for people who didn't come to gamble.

It is interesting to note the average length of stay in the city has increased in recent years, and visitor and gaming revenue figures reveal that average losses on gambling per trip have also increased.

When we discuss individual losses on slots, I like to quote what I call the Rule of 80. Simply stated, the Rule of 80 is my summary of the realities and perils of slot machine play:

♠   80 percent of slot players lose
     80 percent of their money on
     80 percent of their visits

While it is simple to calculate the volume of losses in each area or state from the statistics released by the various state gaming authorities, it is impossible to gauge the number of times specific individuals lost money or the actual amount each person lost during a single visit or over a period of time.

The casinos could tell us how much money was lost on any given day in their establishments, but they cannot keep track of all wins and losses for individual players. They compile a broad range of data on those who use their casino privilege cards and slot club cards but even in the age of sophisticated computer tracking systems such as Oasis, there is no guarantee the information assembled is absolutely accurate. For example, several of my best wins have been on machines which would not accept my card because of temporary problems. Also, though some casinos exchange information on customers from time to time, the record of wins and losses at one place does not carry details on activity elsewhere.

Club cardholders are likely to be more serious players than the casual or first-time visitor. Since cardholders are more likely to spend more hours in the casino, it follows that the average loss among slot club members will be higher than the overall average. At Trump Castle in Atlantic City, for example, the loss per visitor has been quoted at $31 per day but cardholders lose $101 per day, more than three times as much.

When I test the Rule of 80 on slot floor managers and casino executives, some label it an exaggeration but most concede that on any given day the rule probably holds true for their operations.

We know, of course, that the $78.5 billion dollars spent in Nevada in 1993 were not virgin dollars carried into the casinos. They represent a combination of bankrolls and recycled winnings as millions of players take and retake from the slot machine trays and play out the credits that have built up on the meters.

When people bring more of their own money to the casino

they stay longer and that means greater profits for the house. But it is immaterial to management what portion of slot revenues actually comes from new or recycled money. Casinos end up with a cut from every dollar played.

Since the 189 gaming locations mentioned earlier retained $3.685 billion as their combined 1993 win and paid the remainder to their customers in winnings, the net effect of all this activity was that $75 billion in cash was redistributed among the people who risked money.

How much did you get? I finished up with a minuscule percentage because I was one of the fortunates who made money on slots in 1993. But my share would account for very few of the zeros in $75 billion.

Why is it that so few of us win? And apart from those rare big jackpots, why do our winnings seem so small?

It is a complex calculation but it seems more than half the distribution of those so-called *winnings* must have gone back to people who actually *lost* money. Much of the balance represents a return of the cumulative stakes furnished by the winners themselves.

Probably only a small portion of that $75 billion payback could be defined as real winnings which went to people who actually made profits over and above the money they carried into the casino.

The redistribution pool is greater than the gross national product of most states and many countries, but the bulk of those winnings are give backs.

When we play the slots, there is always the remote chance a thunderbolt strike could change our lives forever. But better we lower our sights now and be grateful for slim pickings on the days when we come out ahead of the game.

4

The Odds Are Always
Against You

Be under no illusion. The odds will always be against you.
Playing slot machines, working slot machines, no matter which
term we use or what technique we devise, the chances of
winning are stacked against us today, tomorrow, next year.

Don't be misled by the terminology. The payout banners
claiming 95 percent or 96 percent or even 97.4 percent do not
mean you will have a 95 percent, 96 percent, or 97.4 percent
chance of winning when you play at those particular carousels.

The banners have a quite different meaning. They are not
talking about return *on* investment but return *of* investment.
And, of course, they are not talking about *your* investment in
particular.

Those signs are telling you the casino is retaining a smaller
percentage of what you give it with each pull on a machine with
97.4 percent payouts than where the stated payout is only 95
percent or 90 percent or where no payout claim is made.

In other words, the casino can state without fear of contra-
diction that you may *lose* less at this spot than somewhere else
on the casino floor.

Of course management doesn't want you to interpret its

largess that way. It would much rather you think in terms of having a 95 percent, 96 percent, 97.4 percent, or whatever chance of winning.

Let me give you a simple example. I tell you I will give you 95 percent for every $100 you invest with me. That sounds like a whopping big profit, almost double your money, right?

Wrong! When you give me $100, I give you back $95. That $95 I returned to you isn't profit. You didn't make money on the deal no matter what I tell you. I am the person who made the money—*your* money. The simple fact is you lost $5 and I have $5 I didn't have before.

Now, I don't expect you to be too happy about this but I'm a persuasive kind of guy when I want to be (and promises in casino gambling can be truly seductive). I cajole you into trying your luck again with the $95 you have left and this time I give you back only $90.25.

Go along with my scheme fifteen times and I will have more money than you. Your $100 will have shrunk to $46.33 (or for those of you who are mathematically minded, 46.329 percent of your original $100). Meanwhile, I have accumulated $53.67 I didn't have before. Guess who is having the fun here!

Great deal for me but what about you? What about that 95 percent I promised? Well, what about it? I reckon I'm a good guy. I keep my promises. Just as I said I would, I paid you back 95 percent each and every time you gave me your money. Only trouble is what I was returning was part of your investment, not an addition to the principal amount.

The problem with this scenario is I should have told you I really intended to pocket 5 percent of your investment each time you trusted me with your hard-earned money.

The casinos are more adept at this kind of thing than I am. They vary the protocol a little but the end result is the same. Instead of giving you a fixed 90 percent, 95 percent, 97.4 percent, or whatever back each time you pull the lever or press the button, they play games with you. It's called marketing.

They vary the return, they will even let you make a profit now and again, and no matter how little they give you back, they call the payout winnings. We are all looking for winnings!

Some slot machines are programmed to make a big song and dance about these winnings even when all they are giving you back is a pittance of what you have put into them.

On every visit to a casino, I see people bewitched by the bells and the music. Until I knew better, I thought they had won a jackpot. Now I know that huge win is more likely to be $40.

The sound effects on some modern state-of-the-art slot machines are convincing and can make any payout sound like a fortune. Reality doesn't set in until the winners pause to add up the payouts and deduct their losses. It is a quick way to come back to earth.

Your winnings may come early in a session. You might strike double bars on your first play and get back $50. Hey, you put in only $2. You are $48 up on the deal already. You might think you've died and gone to slot machine heaven, especially if you happen to pick up more dollars a few pulls later. My advice is beware of small mercies!

I said the casinos vary the protocol a little. Well, the truth is that they vary it a lot, often in rather subtle ways. For example, just because the banner above the carousel says 95 percent or 97.4 percent winnings doesn't necessarily mean the machine you are playing has that kind of payback.

Look at the wording on the banner again, this time more carefully. I bet it says something like "up to 97 percent" with "up to" written in letters rather smaller than the rest of the banner. Truth in advertising can be an elusive thing, especially in casinos.

What that sign really means is somewhere in this nest of twenty or more slot machines there is one, and probably only one, programmed to pay out 97 percent of the money it takes in over a period of time. The payback on the other machines may be as little as 83 percent in Atlantic City, even less in Nevada where the gaming commission has, until recently, set no lower limit on the theory that competition will take care of this problem better than regulation.

The trouble is even when you interpret the sign correctly, you won't know which machine is which and I doubt you will have enough money or fortitude (a synonym for stupidity in this context) to survive the period of time necessary to find out.

Casino technicians may know which machine is which and regular players may learn over time, but take it from me, you are unlikely to be able to distinguish one from another.

In all probability, they will look the same to you, especially if the carousel is following the new fashion and grouping like makes and models on all sides.

We can all be fooled. You see some guy nearby strike blue sevens and you just know that has to be the machine with the best payback. You wait till he picks up what is left of his big win and you sidle over casually, hoping nobody else has spotted this treasure chest; after all, you know that all slots players are competing for the same pool of winnings.

Wrong move. You find the sevens on the new machine have vanished along with the lucky player and, to your dismay, when you look back at where you were before, aha! that's where they went. Too late you realize you were right the first time.

It is a sickening feeling we have all experienced. We make what seems to be the right move and then suspect all we have done is build up the booty for the next player.

That is a common misapprehension. The truth is, even when the next play picks up what you are certain should have been your winnings, it is unlikely you would have won that same payout had you stayed there. However, let me keep the explanation of that riddle till later. For now we will stay with the payback percentages.

To further complicate matters, the slot machines in the

modern casino are technological marvels (or monsters if you prefer). They may look like modern versions of the old, traditional styles, even to the cherries, bars, and sevens, but they are not. No longer can the odds of winning be calculated by simply finding the number of stops on each reel and multiplying that figure (probably twenty, twenty-two, or twenty-four) by three for a three reel machine or by four or five for a wider-body slot.

I have been amazed and appalled to read in several recent books and publications that some writers continue to measure win chances in terms applicable only to older slot machines.

At least two books published within the last year talk about 20 or 24 stops per reel to the power of three and give the odds for a maximum payout as one in 8,000 or one in 13,824 spins for a three reel machine.

This is not so. It wasn't always true of the older style slots. The true odds of hitting any specific symbols combination have always been a function of the number of stops per reel and the number of times the symbol appears on each reel. The chances of hitting three bars are less than hitting any bar simply because there are many more chances of hitting mixed bars, cherries, blanks, or whichever symbols denote smaller payouts on your chosen machine.

Furthermore, payback percentages are not limited to a single complete pay cycle but to a number of cycles. Rather than hit the nominated percentage over one cycle of eight thousand or 13,824 spins, the modern machine will probably work on a payout verification closer to thirty thousand spins, maybe more.

The slot machines you see in casinos today are sophisticated computers, each programmed for a particular type game. As with other computers, what you see is nothing more than a box housing the hardware to run one or more of the software programs produced by the machine manufacturer.

The odds of winning vary even among versions of the same

program, depending on the specifications given when the machine is ordered or at some later date should the casino decide to update the game program.

Most modern machines can host several different game programs offered by the equipment manufacturer. A Haywire two coin machine can become a Home Run or Double Dollars unit overnight merely by changing the name glass, header board, reel strips, and program chip. In today's casino environment, a wild card machine can become a simple multiplier or literally any one of the alternative games the manufacturer is holding in its extensive library of programs.

This is not to suggest game changes are made to confuse or deceive slot players or for any other sinister reason.

We have probably all heard those stories about winning machines being adjusted by casino technicians or similar remedies being applied to beat slot customers down. Ignore those fallacies. Anybody passing on that kind of tommyrot is showing his or her ignorance of what is really happening in the casinos.

Gaming is a very competitive business. The most successful establishments are those which encourage patronage. Casinos are not in the business of making life tougher for their patrons. With computer odds of striking any combination of stops on the most common sixty-four stop, three reel configuration standing at one in 262,144 and the theoretical possibility the figure could be as high as one in 16,777,216 even on a three reel machine, there is no need to make the situation worse. In fact, the reverse is probably truc.

As the overriding objective for any casino operation is to attract customers and keep them, the more likely scenario is that the prudent slots vice president is seeking game programs and devising sales strategies to lure more players to try their luck, to spend more per spin average, and to stay in the casino for longer periods—in other words, to spend more money.

Changes in the selection of game programs and physical placement of slot machines in casinos arise almost entirely from marketing decisions made with one objective in mind: to enhance revenues.

Casino bosses don't really care who wins or loses. Unless you are using their slot club cards at every session, remain at one machine for a long time, or win enough in one hit to qualify for a hand-carried payout, I doubt any casino knows how you, as an individual, fare on your circuit.

What they monitor closely is the performance of each machine you are playing. Unless they can identify you, however, there is no way they can know you, Tom Brown or Agnes Smith, were the person who picked up that last three bar combination on slot number 5678.

The financial success of casinos is predicated on gross revenue; their money does not come directly from individual unlucky slot players. Instead, they will be watching carefully the casino win or hold—that portion of their wagers players as a group leave in the machines over several full pay cycles.

Casino managers are sensitive to competition and know precisely the percentage they must pay back over full pay cycles to induce customers to stay at the machines for longer periods and to keep coming back, win or lose, to their casino rather than the competitor's.

Casinos rate game programs on the twin measures of player appeal and holdability—the capacity of the slot machine's visual impact and game program to attract and retain players for longer periods.

Casino management receives printouts every day on the financial performance of every slot in the establishment. Should any machine fail to meet the activity criteria set down by the casino, the profits from that particular machine will fall short of targets, the slot will likely be put on a watch list, and soon moved elsewhere or switched out.

In most cases, switching means converting newer machines to another game program rather than replacing the slot itself. It could also mean upgrading to a higher payout version of the same or a similar program to ensure there is enough money flowing back to players to encourage them to continue spending.

Higher payout here does not refer to the amount of the top line payout. I am commenting on the overall payback from the game program. The jackpot amount is definitely an indicator of the likelihood of striking that big win, but it works differently than most people think.

Top line payouts of ten thousand coins are alluring but they are less likely to actually reward your efforts than a machine of the same type featuring a top payout of only five thousand or even one thousand coins.

The slot machine strategies I outline later in this book are based on winning from the overall game programs, not from striking top line payouts.

Jackpot wins are few and far between. To date, I have struck a 10,000 coin payout, with three coins in, only once. Yet I win money consistently.

There must be a lesson here.

Which brings us to the subject of the second part of this chapter: human behavior.

- Human behavior is important to the casino because management factors this intangible but reliable imperative into its marketing techniques and profit calculations.
- It is important to the player because most times he or she is blissfully unaware of the impact his or her behavior can have on the end results of a casino visit to Las Vegas, Atlantic City, the nearest Indian Reservation, or the riverboat which has recently tied up at the wharf downtown.

I may surprise a lot of people when I insist human behavior plays a greater part in losing than the actual payback percentages on the slot machines.

To say most of us work hard at the business of losing would

be a gross understatement. It doesn't make sense but it happens every day, in every casino, all over this land.

WE PLAY TO LOSE

If statistics prove the odds are already stacked against us, why would we do this? It doesn't make sense. Yet we do it. The answer to this paradox is that few of us realize what we are actually doing when we try our luck.

Those of us who get the message either abandon casinos as a hopeless cause or promise ourselves we will act differently next time; then, when the opportunity comes along again, we make the same mistakes.

In my opinion, both reactions are wrong.

Don't blame the casinos for your bad luck. They are mostly up-front; they make no secret that they want you, and will encourage you, with a host of seducements, to spend more money than you intended.

They make it easier for you to lose by inducing you to stay past your winning moments, luring you with the promise of richer wins to come, perhaps only a spin away!

Should you run out of ready cash, they conveniently locate ATMs you can use to access your credit card to finance the mad chase for those elusive blue sevens, jokers wild, or red, white, and blues.

Many readers will recall those colorful full-page and half-page advertisements for Vegas World a few years ago. The offers didn't seem to make much fiscal sense for the casino: $398 for a two-night, three-day vacation for two and, when you arrived, Vegas World would give back your money (or more) in cash or casino action and hand out gifts which could exceed $1,000 in perceived value.

Despite his reputation as a high roller, gained from winning a million dollar wager on the outcome of a Super Bowl some years back, Bob Stupak, owner of Vegas World and a member of the group operating the Stratosphere Tower, is a businessman first, a gambler second.

His offers make a lot of marketing sense simply because he knows from long experience that most of those who take him up on his deals will spend the casino action or the cash he has returned to them (their own cash, remember, and he has had the use of it for several months interest free). No matter how firm they may be in their resolutions before they make the trip, he is certain they can be relied upon to dip deep into their pockets and come up with yet more money to leave in his casino.

Mr. Stupak also factors in three other vitally important points:

- Those who are lucky enough to win will probably return to Las Vegas next year or the year after and will surely come back to his casino.
- Most of those who lose will do so in good spirits because they think they got a great deal and a free vacation; they, too, are more likely to return to his establishment than the average Joe who visits Las Vegas once, pays for everything out of pocket, and loses his shirt.
- The ratio of winners to losers in these vacation groups will be the same as for any other group of casino patrons.

Mr. Stupak couldn't lose on his Vegas World offers and no doubt we will see similar marketing techniques used to popularize the new Stratosphere Tower. He can't lose, not even when some lucky soul hits the $1 million jackpot he offers. He collected that money from the less fortunate long ago and has it set aside in escrow, probably earning a hefty rate of interest as it waits for the one person in ten million who will strike it lucky and take the booty.

Casino marketing men bet on human fallibilities and it is isn't a gamble. . . it is a sure bet. How many times have you been winning during a session in the casino yet finished up losing?

We have all done this. On many of those occasions, we know we should have taken more money away than we brought in but we didn't. We finished up losing money. How did this happen? The answer is right with us: human behavior!

In the excitement or the torment of the moment, when it really counts, people are affected by the atmosphere in a casino and the compulsion to keep trying their luck. We don't think everything through in a rational way. We decide this is *our* day, or we just know this next pull or the next machine will bring thousands of coins rushing into our slot trays. We see sevens everywhere except where they should be—on the pay line—and we convince ourselves it is only a matter of time before they will start coming our way.

The trickle of small payouts on slot machines can be mesmerizing. The casinos rely on this. They know most patrons, their hunger whetted with tantalizing small wins, will continue playing until they start losing again.

It is as though we have been programmed to believe it is beneath our dignity to depart the premises while we are winning. Of course, that isn't the way we think. But unhappily, for our pocketbooks and our humor, it is the way most of us behave.

An example: I was in Las Vegas prior to a Thanksgiving weekend a few years ago, moving around my chosen machines and making money steadily. The night before the holiday, two couples began playing a slot beside one of my stops, taking turns and working in two- to four-hour shifts to cover twenty-four hours per day over a three-day period.

They brought in several thousand dollars—my guess is at least $10,000—and were clearly in a winning mood, high on expectations but, in my experience, low on common sense.

I watched their ricocheting between wins and losses for most of the time they were there. As I saw them only when I came to the adjacent machine, about ten times over the three days, I witnessed little actual play but talked with them often and occasionally took a moment to stand by and watch.

I built up an acquaintance, especially when the group realized my tour brought me back regularly and I won consistently from a small investment and restricted play, whereas their fortunes fluctuated wildly and, for the most part, miserably.

They ended up losing most of their stake, almost an inevitable conclusion to their long weekend. I anticipated the likely outcome early on and, although I make it a policy not to give advice to other people when I am in a casino, I had several discussions about their tactics with one of the men in the group and did my best to persuade him to reconsider their game plan.

He would have none of it, even when I pointed out they would have to strike gold and win the top line, with three coins in, just to recover the amount of money they had elected to risk on this single machine.

When I did a mathematical calculation to show him that, in all likelihood, they were virtually guaranteed to lose at least 80 percent of their stake the way they were playing, he conceded the probable accuracy of my figures but insisted they might strike it lucky anyway and win the big one before they ran out of money.

Here were two professional couples, educated and affluent people who, without realizing it, had become united in their determination to lose their money.

And lose it they did.

At one stage late in the game, after it finally became apparent even to them that this was going to be a very costly weekend, the other man in the group commented to me that at least they had paid for their accommodations and meals with their volume of play.

I told him they would have to be the most expensive rooms and meals in Las Vegas.

I offer one more example before we leave this section. This time it concerns a man who did win the top line payout—

$10,000 with all coins in—on a Black Gold machine at the Riviera.

I spotted this man early in the morning. He was bleary-eyed and unshaven and had apparently been there throughout the night. Two of the machines I was working were nearby on the same carousel. Thus I was in a position to see what he was doing, but I didn't pay particular attention to him until the next morning when, there he was, even more dishevelled and dog-tired, still at the same machine.

My curiosity aroused, I questioned him. He told me he had come to Las Vegas on a family vacation and he had not intended to risk much money on gambling. However, he had struck it lucky immediately. Three or four days before, he had hit a 10,000 coin jackpot in the first few minutes of what was supposed to be his only session at the slots.

Buoyed by this exciting win, he and his wife had agreed he should "follow the lucky streak," as he put it. He had tried several other slots in the casino without much success and so had elected to return to his winning machine. He was determined to stay there until he struck it rich again.

Needless to say, he didn't strike it rich. He lost a lot of sleep and a lot of money. In fact, when my companion and I talked with him, he had managed to reduce his winnings to less than $1,500. He quit not long after we spoke and volunteered as he went by that he had lost yet another $200.

The example of the relay group supports my contention that, although it is important you be adequately funded before you enter any casino, never risk more than you are likely to win.

This second man reinforces another axiom—take your winnings and leave. Don't stretch your luck. Just when you think it may be elastic, it will more likely break than expand.

Remember, here was a man who had won the biggest single-hit payout possible in that casino for a stand-alone dollar slot. Yet, instead of taking the money and heading home, he and his wife decided they could win more. Foolhardy!

In both these situations, the only winner was the casino. Unfortunately, these are not isolated cases. Slot players are making the same mistakes, to a greater or lesser extent, every day.

It is great for the casinos. They predicate a large portion of their profitability on the certainty that their patrons will react to good fortune and bad alike in an emotional rather than a logical way.

Let's restore some balance to this equation. Common sense and self-discipline can reward us with a share of those profits. We can learn that it is possible to leave the casinos with all the money we brought with us and our winnings too. It's not always easy, and we cannot logically expect to do it every time, but it can be done.

5

Players Lose— Workers Win

Remember the man who said he was working? I make no apologies for repeating it yet again—he was working, working methodically, and working hard.

It was a lesson I have learned well. My own experiences and field experiments since meeting that slot machine guru have reinforced his message time after time.

Since that early morning chance meeting, I have seen him only once, about four years ago. At that time, he was staying with his successful strategy. On that night at least, he was still winning, an admission he conceded with characteristic reluctance.

Recently I went looking for him again only to find that he is, apparently, no longer pursuing his slots circuit in Las Vegas. An employee at the casino where I first met him told me there was a rumor he had bought a business out of town but nobody really knew for sure.

For what it is worth, I doubt he would have departed voluntarily to play slot machines someplace else. Better the devil you know, as the saying goes.

With his accumulated winnings, maybe he did buy a

business or earn enough to spend the rest of his life in a more tolerable and comfortable way.

Make no mistake. Extracting a regular income from slot machines is by definition a virtual impossibility. At best it would be a tough nerve-racking life. Few people would have the mental discipline and intestinal fortitude to succeed, let alone persevere for any prolonged period of time to continue that success. I know for certain I could never do what that Working Man was doing each and every week, week after week.

In my research for this book, I have crossed the trail of only one other man who was able to make better-than-wages profits from slots.

His story did not end so well. In a sad way, it again emphasizes the importance of bringing a work ethic to this activity, maintaining it at all times, and establishing guideline parameters which will automatically terminate losing runs before any real damage can be done.

This gentleman was accustomed to visiting Las Vegas much the way I do now, several times each year. Like mine, most of his excursions over a period of several years were successful; unlike mine, some of his visits were generating five-figure profits.

When he totaled his winnings and realized he was $75,000 or more ahead, he decided he would be better off financially if he sold his house, moved his family to Las Vegas, and played the slots full-time.

That decision was unwise. Within two years, maybe less, he lost all the money he had won, his house and car were gone, and he finished up working as a mid-level employee in a casino—a far call from the successful slots winner who had departed his hometown, family in tow, with such great hopes.

He had enjoyed a charmed run as a sometime gambler, but he chose to raise the stakes and gambled his all on a perceived ability to keep winning. What he discovered was that the Windows of Opportunity would not open wider merely to reward his loftier ambitions.

Why did one of these men succeed and the other fail? The Working Man was a strategist, disciplined and in control, unlikely to fall into either of the twin abysses which too often envelope the unwary: greed and gambling addiction.

The second player had enjoyed a lucky streak, but was not content to accept his good fortune for what it was...luck. He craved more. He became greedy.

It is a moot point whether that same misfortune would have eventually befallen our Working Man had he continued. I believe it could easily happen if he abandoned his protocol and increased the amount of money at risk each day.

We all know the danger that besets top athletes who go on past their optimum years. Pride gets in the way of reality and they talk themselves into trying to regain those moments when they seemed invincible.

So, too, with gamblers and gambling. If any reader harbors dreams of making slot machines a way of life, I do not recommend it, not as a satisfying occupation nor as a quick route to millions.

Over the past few years I have developed my own strategies and added my own rules to the basic approach I learned from that Working Man. My experiences have confirmed, for me anyway, that there are few shortcuts to beating the slot machines on a regular, day in, day out basis.

Anyone of legal age can play the slots. A university degree is not a prerequisite nor is mechanical skill. You don't have to be a computer whiz or a commercial or residential property owner. You don't even have to be a taxpayer or a U.S. citizen.

The slots are open to all, male and female, young and old, republicans, democrats, and the politically independent, housewives, bus drivers, soldiers, sailors, factory workers, farmers, ranchers, and professional people.

All you need is money. The machines will not ask you where that money came from or whether you can afford to lose. Just keep feeding in those coins. Casino bosses will love you.

Anybody can play, but can anybody win?

Good question! I'll try to answer it as best as I can.

If you are not prepared to do your homework, to develop or adopt a strategy, to risk an adequate stake you can afford to lose, or to stick with your game plan when the machines are coming up empty, I suggest there are a hundred better ways to indulge yourself in your leisure time.

If you seek excitement or a way to make your fortune from a combination of brinkmanship and adrenaline, try lion taming instead. Sure, you will need to learn to hold the whip and chair but you will have less competition from other would-be lion tamers, and wild animals may not be quite as dangerous as slot machines to your body and soul, certainly not to your bank account.

I have seen novice players collect a big win on their first or second visit to the casino. That is luck, pure and simple. A single win does not a trend make.

I have seen regular players intersperse steady losses with occasional big wins which send them into ecstasy. Those wins, too, are matters of luck, nothing else.

I have seen usually prudent people who carefully evaluate every expenditure of time, money, and energy in their business and personal lives come to Vegas and start doing things which they would otherwise consider absurd.

Their behavior in the casino virtually precludes all chance they might have of leaving with more cash than they brought—unless they are extraordinarily lucky and hit big in the last hour before they rush for the plane.

Unfortunately, luck is a fickle lover; too often it kisses and runs away. Sooner or later, it will desert you and leave you with little more than a sense of abandonment, battered hopes, and badly bruised confidence. If you enter the casinos relying solely on luck, you are doomed to disappointment.

The inescapable truth in slot machine law is this:

♠ **Winning consistently is hard and often exhausting
work, both physically and mentally.**

If you expect to come out ahead, whether from one session
or a series of sessions, the cardinal rule of a successful business
applies here as anywhere else: Plan your work and work your
plan.

The exercise should start long before you arrive at the
casino. Just because there is a new riverboat casino at the dock a
mile down the road doesn't mean you should spend your money
there. That may be the last place you should visit.

Convenient location can be a dangerous trap. It does not
necessarily follow that the big, shiny slot at the front door of the
casino... you know, the machine with the bright red sporty
convertible on display for all to see and salivate over... is where
you should be risking your hard-earned cash, no matter how
much you might yearn to drive that car into the sunset. Best you
know ahead of time whether you should even be thinking about
walking through the front door of that establishment.

I do not spend money at any casino unless I have collected
as much information as I can about that establishment and have
spent some time surveying what happens on the slot machine
floor.

I restrict my play to certain types of slots and will not be
enticed by bright colors, glorious graphics, sound effects, or
stories of big wins.

I follow a precise pattern of play, cash allocation, and time
allotment when I have made my choice of casinos and machines.

All these are elements of a Managed Luck preparation and,
like my on-site protocol and record keeping, they are necessary
parts of my work plan.

I cannot be certain whether I am going to win on any given
day or how much I may win. What I can anticipate, with
confidence fortified from previous experience, is that I will most
likely win more than I lose over the course of a stay, provided I

am resolute and continue to work my plan no matter what happens during any one machine session or on any given day.

Remember the Working Man's comment when I questioned him about his winning. He said, "You can call it luck. I call it inevitable."

He made an even more significant remark when I said he couldn't control the machines: "No, but I can control me and that's more than half the battle."

He was right, but complete control does not come easy to anybody in the casino environment. There are many times when it can be very difficult to persevere with a game plan, to follow the rules irrespective of the financial pummeling you may be suffering, or to combat the instincts which convince you your run of luck will keep going. That feeling of infallibility can be disastrous.

The gut reaction when you are losing is to quit and conserve what's left of your stake. And, if you let yourself be lured into thinking you are on a lucky streak or the machine is "hot," you are likely to charge ahead and ignore your game plan because things are going so well.

Beware the Ides of March! and April! and May! and every other month! Don't abandon the predetermined strategy no matter the temptation.

I can comment on these dangers because I have spent so much time watching how others behave and because, even after I devised my strategies and began to prove them, my major disciplinary demand was to steel myself against the urge to quit early when losing, or worse, to overstay a winning streak. I had to struggle to stay in control—and still do.

Inclinations, predilections, or compulsions, call them what you will, are a matter of degree. We all have these feelings.

I have from time to time deliberately experimented with losing quick and winning quick. Since I hate losing, the tests were limited in number. I make no apology for that and understand if you consider the results inconclusive or mere coincidence. I do not.

In a total of twenty-one days over four visits to Las Vegas, working at two casinos, three of the five days I lost money were days when I deliberately elected to close early or run with the luck.

One of those days produced the worst beating I have taken from the slots, the only day in six years when I have lost virtually my whole stake.

Even though I was already thinking about writing this book and could perhaps justify additional losses in the name of research, I was not prepared to risk losing more by continuing that experiment.

The remainder of this book will reinforce a number of important messages time and again, themes which are fundamental and critical in devising winning strategies. None will be more imperative than this matter of the attitude you bring to the business of winning, both before you go to casino and when you are there.

You must work to win!

6

Attitude and Affordability

People have different interests and motivations.

One person's excitement may be another's drudgery. I know people who will tell you they cannot stomach sports, yet they are dedicated to racing cars or motorbikes. Since these activities involve mechanical devices, they don't see inconsistencies in their attitudes even though they may concede they are pitted against others in intense competition.

The way they see it, what excites them is a lot different from games where mere humans interact, plowing into each other with hockey sticks, pummeling each other with boxing gloves, or dodging opponents while trying to throw a ball through a hoop. In turn, the baseball fan may be thoroughly bored by a game of football or hockey and wouldn't be seen at a racing event. And the true sports enthusiast, to whom all things competitive are thrilling, could be the one person in a room who doesn't get a kick out of the latest Sly Stallone video.

The graduate student who is into chemistry in a big way may find the fusion of elements in a laboratory experiment far more exhilarating than any sport or leisure activity. The bookworm may wonder why people waste time doing anything else when they could be totally enveloped in the intricacies of a complicated mystery novel or caught up in the vicarious pleasures of a romantic escapade.

There are at least three common factors in determining what is interesting or worthwhile for each of us in choosing our leisure pursuits:

- natural inclination
- knowledge
- accessibility

American football developed from the game of rugby and requires similar running, tackling, and ball-handling skills. It follows that first-class or international rugby players and their counterparts, American football players, have a common motivation and have developed high levels of competence based on abilities they have in common.

These athletes enjoy the one-on-one and team versus team aspects of their sports, the emphasis on individual skills which merge into an interaction with and a mutual dependence on their teammates. They relish the personal physical confrontations they face during games.

The overseas rugby player, however, is not too impressed by American football and National Football League players don't care much for the game played without pads. The reasons are geographical. Neither group has been given the opportunity at a young age to stimulate similar inclinations through knowledge of and exposure to the other sport. Rugby is most popular in countries outside North America while American football is restricted mainly to this continent.

In addition to inclination, knowledge, and accessibility, in gambling there is a fourth influence which often overrides the other three.

Our social institutions and religious tenets tend to condemn gambling, be it betting on greyhounds or race horses, or playing poker, roulette, or slot machines. Not even office sweepstakes escape this denunciation.

Despite a more enlightened outlook generally, and with twenty-six states offering or about to offer casino gambling, some jurisdictions continue to prohibit all games of chance, including office sweeps.

While the laws in many of those areas may be observed more in the breach than in the compliance, they reflect the ambivalence in officialdom toward anything to do with gambling. Other states permit only certain forms of activity or apply rigid regulations which make commercial gaming operations impractical.

From a young age many of us are taught gambling is an insidious disease which destroys individuals, ruins marriages, causes crime, and creates hardship all around.

It is ironic. Our society salutes million dollar salaries for ball players, tolerates the chicanery of stock market manipulators who make fortunes from paper transactions without adding a single unit to our gross national product, and endorses the entitlement of lawyers to an obscene share of court-awarded damages in injury cases. This same society pontificates that gambling is iniquitous, and encourages people to expect something for nothing!

We all know of employers who pay workers minimum wage or less, keep them in factories ten and twelve hours a day, often without overtime payments, and restrict their access to health insurance and other entitlements while amassing huge personal assets for themselves. These people too frequently become civic leaders who will, in good conscience, of course, object vociferously to the introduction of gaming activity in their states, their counties, and their cities.

State governments which advertise their lotteries and scratch-off ticket games on television every day will vigorously campaign against other gambling activities which do not generate revenue share for the official agency.

Churches, which have operated bingo parlors as fund-raisers for years, are loud in opposition to casinos in their area or at the nearby American Indian Reservation.

Curiously, our society, which elevates murderers and other miscreants to celebrity status, in some states allowing them to directly or indirectly profit from their crimes in book and movie deals, becomes alarmed at the prospect that a few hardworking citizens may waste their money at the casino or racetrack in the next state and descend into dependence on welfare or charity.

Apparently it is acceptable to make money with little or no contribution and to profiteer at the expense of others, so long as it is not done through gambling. It is sometimes difficult to identify the distinctions between what is socially correct and what is not. I am hard put to find any great difference between buying options or futures on the commodities markets and taking a flyer at a casino. Both are gambles. The futures buyer can no more control the weather than the slot player can control the machine. Lose either way and your investment is gone.

If we are to put this clamor in its proper perspective, we should acknowledge that, when it comes to gaming, if our state, city, church, or market shares in the spoils, then they do not consider the activity addictive or menacing to society.

The hypocrisy is lost in the rhetoric and the posturing.

Sadly, there is justification for concern. Gambling can be addictive. Gambling can create situations of real personal hardship. Gambling can destroy marriages, threaten lives, and deprive families of necessities and opportunities. This is why there are chapters of Gamblers Anonymous throughout the country. It is an interesting comment on human behavior to note that these chapters are not confined to states where casino gambling is authorized.

Like many other pursuits which can get out of control or are subject to sudden and dramatic changes of fortune, gambling can wreak havoc long before it reaches the addiction stage.

Compulsive gamblers are not the only people who have committed suicide in despair over financial losses and personal crises which should have never been allowed to develop. Wall Street has seen more than its share.

In my opinion, no reader should contemplate any form of gambling unless he or she has first conducted a candid and absolutely honest appraisal of his or her weaknesses and strengths and established an unassailable position on two very important criteria—attitude and affordability.

This is especially true of slots. My approach places an emphasis on the attitude you bring to the machines. This is the foundation of your effort. I believe it would be impossible to develop, follow, and maintain winning game strategies, come what may, unless you are philosophically reconciled to what you are doing.

I recommend a simple and practical attitude test.

Sit down and talk to your spouse or some other person whose opinion you respect or who could in some way be affected by your failure or success. Tell that person what you are considering. Discuss your intentions and do not hide anything. Should you find you are uneasy at the prospect of broaching this subject, don't start gambling.

The main objective in this exercise is not to find out whether the other person will support you in the decision you make. That is another issue. The point is whether you are comfortable enough to discuss with somebody close to you what could otherwise be a contentious issue.

There is another caution. Addictive personalities are entering especially dangerous territory in gambling. If you cannot control your drinking or are susceptible to excessive enthusiasm for hobbies or interests, there is a strong possibility you could be swamped by the rivers of no return when you start gambling.

Few activities are of themselves as seductive and compelling as slot machine play; few offer both the lure of riches and the emotional highs which attend every roll of the reels.

We are looking for winners here, more winners and fewer losers. We must stay with the basics.

Let us assume you have completed honest introspection. You have no hangs-ups or preconceived notions about gambling as a pastime, as entertainment, or as a means of making money. What next?

Affordability. Can you afford to gamble and how much can you afford to risk?

The importance of an adequate stake cannot be emphasized too often. Even given a strong, winning attitude, adequate information, and the opportunity to visit casinos when you wish without disrupting your life, you will get nowhere unless you can fund the visit from monies which are not required for any other purpose.

Embarking on a gambling trip without a dedicated stake is akin to a one-legged man attempting a hundred yard dash. You could win but I wouldn't bet my life on it.

Taking that trip without first determining the amount of money needed to finance your game plan is like a marathon runner starting his race in worn-out shoes with flapping soles. No matter how indomitable your spirit, there is little likelihood of going the distance.

In racing, victory generally goes to the best prepared, mentally and physically. The swiftest doesn't necessarily win the sprint every time, nor is the best-trained and equipped endurance runner always victorious in longer races. Given proper preparation, no distractions, and the power of personal confidence, however, the odds of victory in any event are much improved.

So with slot machines. An essential part of preparation is calculating the stake required for your particular game plan and, more important, establishing beyond dispute that the money is not needed elsewhere. You should be certain losing the whole stake will not create unwanted problems for you or your family.

We have all heard of people who use the rent money or put off paying the light bill so they will have money to wager or spend on something else. My bet is that most of us have done this ourselves at some time or another with unpleasant results.

I liken diverting money to gambling when it is earmarked or needed for other purposes to a builder removing the support beam from one wall of a house to prop up another. Instead of solving one problem, he has created another and the whole structure is in danger of toppling.

There is no way to concentrate on the process of winning when you are worried about replacing your stake if you lose. I defy any person to maintain the mental discipline necessary to win consistently on slot machines under such circumstances.

Again, you could be lucky once, maybe twice, but the midterm and long-term prospects are bleak. Luck is a precious and rare commodity, not frequently found in casinos. Unless you can manage your luck, luck will manage you! And the consequences can be disastrous.

♠ **Take care of family and financial obligations first. The test of affordability is whether you can lose money without creating other problems.**

I always start from the premise that the worst will happen. I could lose my entire stake at the casino today.

This may seem a strange stance for somebody with a winning attitude but, to be successful, it is essential that I do not delude myself. I must be reconciled to the consequences of the most disastrous scenario before I begin.

That way, I know my objectives can not conflict with my responsibilities, the critical issue of affordability is behind me, and I can concentrate wholly on the task at hand.

What one person can afford to gamble can be an unreasonable amount for another to risk. Fortunately, there are ways of addressing this situation. We can adapt our strategies and expectations to our financial capacities without irrevocably damaging our prospects.

Let's take a few examples.

Most people like to take regular vacations and set money aside expressly for this purpose. For families with young children, the destination of choice may be Disney World or a similar spot with fun activities for the kids.

With the recent move toward providing quality entertainment for all ages in Las Vegas, Reno, and in American Indian reservation resort casinos such as Foxwoods in Connecticut—the biggest such complex in the country—and Mystic Lake in Minnesota, families now can combine vacations and gambling trips without spending more money than planned. They may even save or make money on the deal.

I do not have young children but I am careful with travel costs. I plan ahead and find the lowest airfare when I travel to Las Vegas. Occasionally, I use frequent flyer mileage. Other times I combine the visit with a road trip to another destination.

Courtesy of casino slot club and preferred customer cards, I have not paid for a Las Vegas hotel room in years.

For serious or occasional slot players alike, these cards are worth having. I expect to turn my stake over several times during a visit. Provided I remember to insert the card (sometimes easier said than done), my level of activity each trip assures me of complimentary rooms and, at some places, most of my meals.

I am automatically on the list for special occasions, free slot tournaments, etc., which may bring further savings and other perks such as free drinks and shows. As a result, I can live well in Las Vegas, have a great room with all amenities, and enjoy my visits for little or no out-of-pocket expense.

Fortunately the qualification for these freebies is not a function of winning or losing; it is directly related to the volume of gambling activity. Anybody who goes to the casino with an ample stake can earn free rooms, meals, or other giveaways.

Accommodations and meals in most casino cities are cheap anyway, not in quality but in price. For $29 to $39 a night at several casinos you can get a room which would cost $85 to $125 in other tourist or vacation centers.

For those who like to plan ahead, the charges at off-peak times are even lower. I have recently seen rooms at a popular casino advertised at $19.

Slot club cardholders may qualify for special rock-bottom rates, irrespective of activity. One of my target casinos offers rooms at $29 year-round to slot club members. That is a room rate, not a per person charge.

There are many great tour packages, combining air or bus travel with accommodations, often at a big discount from the regular airfare. Some offers, especially for midweek travel, are absolute steals. These are worth searching for but don't take the first one you find. Check out several.

Eating well should be no problem either. At restaurants or buffets inside your selected casino or elsewhere you can savor sumptuous meals of steak, pork chops, chicken, even lobster, for a few dollars.

Many casinos make a policy of subsidizing food and restaurant costs as a marketing ploy. I have been told by reliable sources that Palace Station in Las Vegas loses as much as $250,000 per month on its food service. While I cannot vouch for the accuracy of the claim, I can tell you the food there is tasty, the portions plenty, and the charges token. Any restaurant or food counter at the Palace is worth a visit.

Because of the timing of my slot sessions, I often find myself eating steak and eggs for early breakfast. I have yet to pay more than $5.95. Best price so far—$1.95.

I have enjoyed dinner for as little as 99¢, an all-you-can-eat buffet, and have bought lunch for 65¢.

Apart from the headliner shows, many costly and unsuitable for children anyway, entertainment is available at bargain prices in casino cities.

Free shows include circus acts, medieval-style jousting, pirate escapades, and simulated volcano eruptions. A wide range of family events and activities can cost less than a trip to the movies.

Your entertainment dollar will stretch farther in Las Vegas and other casino destinations than most any place else. More significant, the whole family can have fun without going near the casino floor. Where else can you drive a few miles to see the Hoover Dam, still one of the great man-made spectacles of the world?

Thus, whether you have set aside $500, $1,000, or more for your vacation this year, you could take your family to Las Vegas, Atlantic City, Ledyard, Reno, Mystic Lake, or many gambling resorts and have enough left from your vacation allocation to stake a few sessions at the slot machines.

Apart from the obvious money advantages, this approach also offers other positive benefits and protections for the novice slot player.

With sightseeing or family outings demanding much of your time, you will have more balance in your schedule. Because you are involved in a variety of activities, you will find it easier to stay with your game plan and will be less tempted to spend longer periods at the machines.

Important, too, is perspective. A balanced approach brings its own bonus—fun. You will enjoy yourself more when you restrict the time you spend at the machines.

Strange as it may seem, you will also enhance your winning prospects.

Maybe you haven't been saving for a vacation. Well, there are other ways to create special funds for any purpose.

Most people spend money on restaurant meals or take-outs regularly or they take two cars to the baseball game when one would do. If you are a smoker, you might not miss half a pack a day if the incentive is compelling. Beer costs less purchased at the store than by the glass at the pub down the road.

It is surprising how quickly these small savings add up. One less restaurant or take-out meal a week can save $15 to $20 or more. That money will quickly accumulate. There may be an added benefit. The home-cooked meal may be better for your health.

However you create your stake, again be sure the money you use for slot machines is free and clear of all other demands.

Time your casino visit for the month when your gambling fund reaches the level you need to finance that family vacation and your slot activity. Don't get itchy feet and raid the cookie jar before there is enough money set aside.

Be imaginative in the way you build the stake but do not mislead yourself. Assume you will spend the entire amount one way or another. Carefully think through the consequences of that happening before you risk a quarter on the slots.

Foresight is to be cherished more than hindsight. Should you anticipate financial trouble from a wipeout, forget the idea of gambling or at least postpone your trip until a more propitious time.

A patient long-term approach makes more sense than charging out with too little money or pirating dollars needed for another purpose and hoping for the best. The best will not be enough in either situation.

Managed Luck does not start when you reach the door of the casino. It begins the day you start thinking seriously about slot machines and decide to try them for yourself.

7

The Fundamentals
of Winning

There is a wealth of truth in the old saying winners sometimes lose but losers never win. Gambling is a true test of this philosophy.

I am convinced that, if you go to the casino resigned to the probability you will lose your money, that is precisely what will happen unless you strike a lucky run. You may be fortunate once or twice but I predict that for most of us the tide will stop rising before Lady Luck kicks in in any significant way.

It would be pointless, misleading, irresponsible to rule luck out as a critical factor in gambling. It is the same in golf, employment, and most other life pursuits.

Winning the lottery is an example of incredible luck because there can be no other explanation when the odds are so stacked. But winning that important prestige job, against a dozen applicants with similar or better qualifications, is also an example of how luck works in the real world.

As with a win in the lottery, that kind of luck can change the course of your life. You may have stepped onto the fast track but had you been one of the less fortunate candidates you would still be job hunting, perhaps in a market where there may be many others with similar skills and training but precious few opportunities.

One step onto the fast track and one stroke of luck do not make a career. The ambition you bring to your new occupation, and your actual performance, will combine to determine your future promotions and the degree of overall success you are likely to enjoy.

So, too, with gambling. You may not have to contend with others for that slot machine seat but, while luck may be a factor in determining the amount of money you win when you are there, other aspects of your approach and working protocol are likely to have a greater bearing on your capacity to win money regularly or lose less over time.

For that reason, I am inclined to discount luck. I see it as the seductive unknown which may determine whether the symbol combinations you hit most often today are blue sevens or double bars. If you are lucky, great, but don't count on Lady Luck too much or too often—you will be disappointed.

The similarities between gambling and professional golf are intriguing. The golfer brings to the course what is, to most of us duffers, an incredible level of skill, experience, and dedicated practice. Yet, on any given day, no matter how well the golfer applies those attributes, success more often than not will come down to whether a drive travels a yard too far in the air, hits a side slope, and cannons into the rough, instead of finishing in the fairway.

Even great putters like Jack Nicklaus, Bob Charles, Ben Crenshaw, and relative newcomer Phil Mickelson have periods when the ball seems to have a mind of its own and keeps lipping out.

They do not change their approach simply because some days the drives fly straight and the putts drop into the cup and on others they don't. The great golfers study the courses, persevere in practice (more so when luck is running against them), and keep to their game plan.

They know the more knowledge and skill they bring to their rounds the more likely they are to win, whether their luck is good or bad. If the ball doesn't drop today, as long as they persist in their game plan and apply their skills, they will be positioning themselves to win. Sooner or later that ball will start dropping, if not today, tomorrow or the next day or at the next tournament.

Pro golfers talk about game management and course management. My slot machine approach is luck management.

I work on the theory that my luck will most often be bad. For that reason, I must first do my homework and prepare myself properly. If I am not willing to do the work, I shouldn't risk a single dollar. Simple as that.

In an earlier chapter, I stressed the importance of the adage "plan your work and work your plan," and how this should become a maxim for serious slot machine players.

Any person who really wants to do better at the slots should consider *work* and *plan* more than keywords for success. The words can also be acronyms for the fundamental points of winning. If there is only one phrase you remember from this book, let it be this:

PLAN YOUR WORK

Plan before you go to the casino. Work your plan when you are there.

Moreover, the letters which spell these words also can represent elements I consider vital if you are to bring Managed Luck to bear on your slots activities and turn losing days into winning days.

First, let's look at the word *plan*:

P for Planning and Preparation
L for Loss Limits
A for Adequate Stake and Affordability
N for Number of Casino Visits,
      Number of Days per Visit,
      Number of Sessions per Day,
      Number of Spins per Session

In previous chapters, we have discussed the need for proper *Planning and Preparation* before visiting a casino. In a later chapter, we will talk about choosing casinos and slot machines.

A vital element in any plan is determining whether or not you should even consider risking money on slots.

Should you decide this is what you want, you must satisfy all the other elements of P–L–A–N before your preparations will be complete.

Your planning should be appropriate for the level of activity you anticipate. Ponder your approach from the short- and midterm view, devising the strategies you will apply on a daily and per visit basis.

Everybody should set *Loss Limits*. The level may differ from one person to another but the importance does not. To retain full control at all times and work your strategy, you need guidelines.

There is a distinction between the amount of your daily stake and your total loss limit. While I am prepared to lose my daily stake, I am not willing to lose the sum total of my daily stakes over a full three day visit.

The game plan I use most, an aggressive strategy on dollar slots, has a daily stake of $600. For a three-day visit, my theoretical bankroll is $1,800.

Although I expect to win each day I am in a casino, I am reconciled to the possibility of losing my entire stake for that day. Thus, $600 is my daily loss limit.

My limit per visit, however, is not three days at $600 per day (or $1,800); it is $1,200, the equivalent to a complete wipeout on two consecutive days. So far, I have not come close to my maximum loss limit on any visit.

Further, in any given year, I expect to make three to six visits to Las Vegas. Irrespective of the frequency of visits, I have set my annual loss limit at $3,000.

At first glance, these may seem paradoxical positions to take. If I am ready to risk $600 per day on each of three days, why am I not prepared to lose $1,800 over a three-day visit or more than $3,000 in a year?

There are two answers, one strictly financial, the other basically strategic. Both are vitally important.

I have calculated my average win. While I have made more than a thousand dollars per day or per visit several times, a typical amount is more likely to be around $150 to $400 on a winning day and $300 to $800 over a three-day visit.

Were I to lose my entire stake on the first day of a three-day visit, I would still have a fair chance of coming out a winner overall or, at worst, suffering an acceptable loss.

Losing my limit on two consecutive days would make that recovery goal more difficult but it remains within reach. Set the loss limit per visit higher, however, and I can just about guarantee that at some time I would probably lose more than I could recover next time around, or maybe from the next two or three visits combined.

Instead of keeping somewhere ahead of the game, I would have let myself fall so far behind that the potential profit for my entire year would be at risk.

I am not prepared to do that and, fortunately, my resolve has not been tested either on a per visit or an annual basis.

My preplanned strategy determines my actions in the casino—which brings us to the second reason I have not encountered this problem. My game plans have a built-in defense mechanism.

When I have a really bad day, or my accumulated losses over

two days come uncomfortably close to my loss limit for a whole visit, I change my game strategy from an aggressive approach to a capital conservation plan, as in Work Plan One, which I detail toward the end of this book.

In so doing, I am deliberately trading the potential for higher returns for a policy of protecting my stake. Put in more earthy terms, I am scurrying to cover my backside. The defense works well.

Please take note of this. A correction device built into your game plan is critical. When I make this switch, I am not abandoning my original strategy, but I am moving to another "what if" part of the program.

Before we leave Loss Limits, there is another point to stress. Leave your credit cards and checks at home. This caveat is important now and it is about to become more so.

In recent years automatic teller machines have been placed in most casinos. The amount of money being taken from these machines on an average day far exceeds the most optimistic expectations of the executives who dreamed up the idea of having readily available sources of cash for their patrons.

The result is that many people lose far more than they could otherwise. Convenient access to ATMs, and credit cards or bank cards in your pocket, spells DANGER in capital letters. Your loss limit resolutions are likely to go out the window in a flash.

If the location of ATMs inside casinos was a brilliant move, the next switches are devilishly ingenious... card-swipe devices attached to slot machines. The first versions, already approved in some jurisdictions, accept prepaid house debit cards. The next step—financially ominous—is but a minor modification away as these units have the in-built capacity to provide direct access to available credit card balances.

Most modern slots have bill changers. Insert your $5, $10, or $20 note, the paper money is converted into slugs or quarters. These devices work better for the casino than for patrons because they keep players locked into one machine for longer periods.

Oh, what we pay for the luxury of convenience! Imagine what direct credit card access could mean for you; instead of using cash carried into the casino, you will be able to insert your card and play straight off your credit line.

For far too many people, their available credit card balances will vanish quicker than they can read the digits.

Do not tempt fate. Set your loss limits before you go to the casino. Take your stake in cash.

We have devoted a full chapter to the issue of *Affordability*, to ensuring the stake you allocate for slot machine play is no more than you can afford to lose.

But we have not discussed the amount of money you should have in that stake. In the outlines of the various work plans, I nominate amounts required to operate each plan effectively. Let's look at some other key guidelines.

I have mentioned that I fund my dollar slot activities with a $600 daily stake which I have found adequate for my more aggressive game plans. Nonetheless, this could be considered a mid-range figure for a dollar player simply because, no matter which of my various strategies I choose, I always use a measured investment protocol and restrict my sessions to two coin machines.

For three coin slots, I believe I would need a daily stake of no less than $800, maybe $1,000. That is reason enough to shun three coiners, apart from my conclusion that it is more difficult to maintain a winning record when more money is at risk— points I will discuss in more detail in the chapter on the various types of slot machines.

Conversely, I have found I can finance a full day's activity, following one of my capital conservation game plans, with a much smaller stake. While the Green Plan calls for a fixed investment of $600, I have found most times I can finance the whole day on around $200 and still put the full $600 through over the slate of twelve machine sessions. Most of the money is recycled from the earlier sessions, as I cash out frequently.

Having said that, I am firm in my conviction that the amount of the stake you can afford to lose should determine the denomination of the slots you work.

I do not advocate jumping from quarters to dollars or vice versa in the course of a day or even during a full visit. You should be adequately funded for one or the other at the outset, then stay with that denomination.

Unless you can allocate at least $500 or $600 to a daily stake, you should avoid dollar machines altogether and concentrate on the quarter slots where your stake should be no less than $150 and certainly no more than $200 for any of the game strategies I outline.

Don't look to me for a recommendation of a stake figure for nickel machines. This is not because I am against nickel slots per se. I am against the way they are set up.

Nickel machines are big winners for the casino. I have yet to find a location where the game programs on the nickel slots are as user-friendly as they are on quarter or dollar slots.

Rather than indicate an appropriate stake for nickel play, I suggest you delay that casino visit until you have built an affordable fund for either dollar or quarter slots. Your patience could bring a handsome reward.

Now we come to the *Numbers*—days per visit, sessions per day, spins per session, even the number of dollars you should risk at each session.

Note that what I call a session is the time spent at a single machine; a day is made up of a specific number of sessions, and a visit will comprise so many days. These are a vital part of your planning and should be decided before you leave home. These numbers are the core of your strategy.

Each of the work plans included in this book has a preset number of spins or coins per session and a specific number of sessions for a full day's activity.

These numbers are not chosen at random. They are the net result of what could be called applied research.

The results of my field experiments suggest that, on the machines I work, the numbers correlate to the Windows of Opportunity better than most other combinations and thus generate my best and most consistent winning results.

I set up a slots circuit in a single casino or between two locations. The factors common to each of my strategies are:

- Allocation of a fixed number of coins or spins per session
- Definition of a work protocol at each slot
- Continuous movement around the circuit until the day's activity is completed

Let's start with the number of coins and spins per slot.

The numbers in the work plans are based on my assessment of the pay frequencies on target machines and my experience with the average amounts (if there is such a thing) of each payout during the Windows of Opportunity.

Basically, I am looking to cover three pay frequency turns at each machine. That doesn't mean I will get three payouts for say forty coins in or forty spins. Sometimes, I might get six, seven, or eight, other times one or two. The key is that the typical hit rate should be three to four per slot session.

Which brings us to what I call my Two to One Theory. This applies to all phases of the strategies. My own results show a marked similarity in the progressions at all levels.

On average, to return a true profit for a sequence there will be two small or losing payouts for each win which recovers the coins invested over the previous ten spins or since the previous payout.

A return of coins played is not a payout in my book. A cherry or a blank may return two coins for two coins in. All you have is your money back for that spin only. These dribbles are nothing more than casino window dressing. They do not influence my purse, my protocol, or my payout frequency analysis.

In turn, I expect to have two losing or break-even machine sessions for each winning session.

Taking this a stage further, on a three-day visit I could have two losing days to one winning day.

The trick is to limit the amount of losses during the losing sessions and buy enough play with your stake to have a reasonable expectation of winning more from your winning payouts, sessions, and days to cover your losses and make an overall profit.

Using my Green Plan as an example, a full day comprises twelve machine sessions, about one-and-three-fourths to two-and-one-half hours in time. The money allocation per machine is 50 coins.

On a typical day, I will lose at seven or eight of the machine sessions and win on the others. I would be astonished if I lost my entire allocation at any session. That is always a possibility but it has not happened to me yet.

The average loss will be about 20 to 25 coins, or 40 percent to 50 percent of the money at risk during those losing sessions.

Although the losses will vary, the results over the years reveal a remarkable consistency. In any group of seven to eight losing sessions, there will be two or three bigger losses, say twenty-five to forty coins, but the remainder will be small, between one and twenty coins.

Maybe not so coincidentally, the wins follow the same pattern: From four to five winning sessions, there will be one or two good hits and the others bring in just a few coins.

Herein lies the crux of winning regularly and losing less.

More often than not, I can trace my daily winnings to the return from a single session. My goal is to position myself, without overspending, to achieve the one worthwhile win which will recover the losses for the day and reward me with a profit for my efforts.

My results show that the Two to One Theory applies to the size of the wins as well as the losses—there will be two or three insignificant wins for each bigger return.

From a full activity day of about two and a half hours, with an average of eight losing and four winning sessions, I should have enough winners to give me an acceptable mathematical probability that at least one of those wins will be large enough to offset the losses.

Twelve to fifteen machine sessions per day seem to represent the parameters of the Windows of Opportunity.

If I were working a smaller number of sessions, the chances of getting that single decent win would be reduced dramatically. There would not be enough wins to consistently generate the ratio.

With more than fifteen machine sessions in a day, we run into another danger. Since we are logging losing sessions twice as quickly as winners, the more we clock the greater the likelihood the losses will be bigger and will wipe out our wins.

Taking my last three days using the Green Plan as an example, the points I have stressed come through loud and clear.

Day One	Session Count:	5 wins, 7 losses
	Biggest Loss:	$ 40
	Smallest Loss:	$ 4
	Biggest Win:	$122
	Smallest Win (2):	$ 5 each
	Profit for Day	$162
Day Two	Session Count:	4 wins, 8 losses
	Biggest Loss:	$ 34
	Smallest Loss:	$ 16
	Biggest Win:	$116
	Smallest Win:	$ 14
	Loss for Day	$ 20
Day Three	Session Count:	4 wins, 8 losses
	Biggest Loss:	$ 31
	Smallest Loss:	$ 1
	Biggest Win:	$464

Smallest Win:	$ 19
Profit for Day	$363

On this sequence, I was fortunate to enjoy two winning days and an overall profit atypical of that particular strategy; the Green Plan is, after all, first and foremost a capital preservation system.

The previous occasion I used the Green Plan I had two losing days ($117 and $74). My winning day ($76) did not recover the losses but the total deficit over three days, $115, was less than 20 percent of my daily stake. I consider that a satisfactory result for a losing visit.

Going back two visits, the three-day scores were a $79 loss, a $195 win, and a $46 loss for an overall profit of $70, about the norm for a defensive strategy of this type.

The numbers we have discussed here—numbers of coins, numbers of sessions, number of days per visit—are critical aspects of your preliminary planning.

We have not discussed the number of casino visits. This goes back to personal motivation. Are you looking for more fun from your slot excursions or is your objective covering costs and making money?

I believe your first goal should be to win more often and lose less. That spells F–U–N to me. Nonetheless, should you get really serious about this slot machine thing, I strongly recommend you also apply the Two to One Theory to your visits. Build a fund large enough to finance a minimum of three, maybe four, test visits, whether these be to a distant casino or to one within a reasonable drive of home.

Your plan cannot be complete until you have arrived at the numbers which make sense for your situation. The numbers intrinsic to the various work plans in this book work for me. The same philosophical approach should work for you.

However, the numbers cannot work alone. You must also attend to the other aspects of planning addressed in this chapter: Loss Limits and Adequate Stake and Affordability.

Take one element away and you have no P–L–A–N and no reasonable expectation of winning more and winning often.

Now, the word *work*:

W   for Winning Attitude
O   for Order and Control
R   for Record Keeping
K   for Knowledge and Information

A *Winning Attitude* is absolutely imperative to success. Being a thrifty soul, I know well that I would be incapable of suffering even small losses without the confidence that I will win out overall.

A day in the casino is not like a day in the library. One moment you will be winning, the next you are not. If you are like me, you will need the certainty of success to enable you to stick to your strategy through the down times.

I am not sure how a person with a negative disposition can change the way he or she thinks. But I am sure a casino is no place for a person who does not have a positive mental attitude.

There are more than enough moments in any session, or sequence of sessions, to test our resolve, without starting out as losers.

You must have *Order* in your approach and control of your strategy. All the planning in the world will go for naught unless you follow your chosen procedures and stay in control at the casino.

Self-discipline may be an endangered practice in our modern world but it is the ultimate test of Managed Luck.

Nobody can foresee every situation. At best, an effective game plan will reduce the casino edge but it is only as strong as your resolution to stay with it.

The need for order and control applies to virtually every aspect of the work regimen. It is not enough to arrive at the casino with an adequate stake and a winning game plan, essential as these may be.

There should be order in the way you handle your money, e.g., keeping payouts from each session separate from your investment fund.

You must control your emotions and stay focused on the task at hand through each session. When the going gets rough, you must have the conviction and discipline to stay with your plan.

Records are essential for the proper conduct of virtually every human activity, be it business, personal, sports, or leisure. Imagine playing golf without a scorecard. You wouldn't know where you were at any stage of the game.

So, too, with slot machine activity. You need records to enable you to better control your work, to determine which strategies are working for you and which machines are generating results, and to document wins and losses for tax purposes.

In chapter 11 we have printed a sample page from the daily activity record form I use. Whether you adopt this diary or some other record-keeping device, have it with you on every casino visit and use it every day you are there.

Record the results of each session as soon as it ends while it is still fresh in your mind. Do not wait until the end of the day and rely on memory. Remember, there can be no real money or strategy management without timely and accurate record keeping.

The bottom of each page is reserved for an activity summary and observations—which brings us to *Knowledge*.

We will never know everything about ourselves or our pursuits but we cannot afford to let up in our quest to fortify ourselves with as much information as we can before we start a gambling program. The adage that knowledge is power especially holds true when we make informed decisions before taking risks.

Gathering information does not stop at the casino door. We can learn more every day, and we must be vigilant.

Casinos are places of constant change. What is true of one location today may be out-of-date tomorrow, next week or next month.

Some readers may wonder why, with few exceptions, I avoid discussing slot machines by name. The reason is simple. The changing environment within casinos, and the intense competition, mandate that current game programs and machine names will continue to change frequently, that slot machines with new and exotic features will appear, and many existing machines, including some of the more popular, will be swapped out.

The pace of technology in slots is accelerating. Make it your business to know what is going on, not only with your target machines but with other slots as well. Who knows when or where opportunities may emerge to help you balance Managed Luck and Lady Luck.

Winning consistently in any endeavor comes from a combination of preparation and action.

Filling the tank with gas, checking the oil, and pumping the tires will not get you to the end of any journey, no matter how well mapped. They won't even get you started until you turn on the ignition, put the car into gear, and push the accelerator.

Knowing where you want to go will not take you anywhere unless you first know where you are starting from and what you need to get there. Then you must travel the right roads.

So, too, with the fundamentals of winning.

♠ Plan your work and work your plan

Familiarize yourself with the acronyms we've discussed. They are the signposts at the crossroads on your way to more rewarding experiences—and more fun.

8

Setting Your Personal Goals

In any activity, it makes sense to know where you are, why you are participating, and where you are going.

Most businesses have five-year plans which identify goals, strategies, and milestones. The aspiring Olympian knows how much he must improve before team selection. The navigator must plot course and verify position regularly as the ship sails on toward its ultimate destination.

Successful gamblers are not much different. To succeed consistently over the long haul, gamblers must recognize the complexity of the task and know enough to take as much of the chance out of the game as possible. They must have both a game plan and a series of benchmarks to guide them to winning goals which are realistic given the amount of money at risk and the number of times they are exposed to the probability of losing.

For most of us who play slot machines, the prospect of winning even once, let alone consistently, is little more than a pipe dream. We should acknowledge this and reconcile ourselves to the realities before we decide what we can logically expect to win.

The adage which says "if you don't expect much, you won't

be disappointed" applies double to slots. Don't pyramid a small win today into imagined riches next time around. Gambling fortunes have this crazy habit of tantalizing us from the neverland of our tomorrows rather than emerging as cash we can touch and feel today.

That does not mean we should not set goals. We should. Goals should be a vital part of our strategy, but it is important that those goals make sense for us, given our personal circumstances. After all, while $2,000 profit may be a fair target for a high roller going into a card game with $5,000, it would be a flight of fancy for a player starting with $10. Miracles could happen but, if we depend on them, we are doomed to crushing disappointments.

Better to be thrilled by a bigger win than expected than end the day dissatisfied because you won only $200 when you had been coveting $2,000.

I have won $200 many times and been elated. It does not take a genius to figure what my reaction would have been had my daily goal been $2,000 on those days instead of a modest $150.

Unlike the navigator who has one end destination for a journey, slots players can have a mix of goals and reach them all—provided all are realistic.

I have three goals which have proved attainable for me. I am convinced the first two can be achieved by all slot players. The third may prove a little more elusive but, with the right game plan and the fortitude to keep with that plan, it is reachable. These goals can work as well for other people as they do for me. In order of importance, they are: more fun, fewer losses, and realistic profits.

Enjoyment is the product of knowledge and confidence. If we know how to do something properly and have honed our skills to the stage where we can move with a measure of certainty, we will enjoy ourselves more than the person who is unfamiliar with the rules and unsure of the consequences.

The cardinal rule in leisure activities should be enjoyment. If we cannot be happy doing something, we should look for another hobby or pursuit. Would you take up skydiving if you were afraid of heights? Probably not, but skydiving can be the height of fun for many enthusiasts.

The rule applies to slot play, too. Unless it is enjoyable and you can be enthusiastic, why do it? A craving for profit is no valid reason. Have you noticed that the people who succeed in any field are generally those who are happiest in what they are doing?

There is a lesson there.

When you skydive, you may rent equipment and pay a club fee, to but you do not risk losing your shirt financially. You know the costs up front which means you do not have to worry about finding more cash because the winds blew from the southwest instead of the north.

With slot machines, if the winds of fortune blow against you and you have not taken proper precautions, you can easily lose your shirt along with your wallet. I venture to say the majority of people who visit casinos and play slots finish up losing more than they expected—which tends to dampen their fun and temper their enthusiasm.

The work plans in this book are primarily defensive strategies. Even the most aggressive is designed to minimize both the amount and frequency of losses.

They are devised as safeguards against the **Rule of 80**. How much fun can there be in losing 80 percent of our bankroll 80 percent of the time?

By first establishing how much you can afford to risk and taking no more than that into the casino, you will limit the size of any potential loss. Leave credit cards and check books at home.

You can have the most appalling day, but it is impossible to lose more than your daily limit if that is all you have brought along and you have taken steps to ensure there are no sources of instant money available should your discipline crack.

By adopting a defensive game plan and following a strategy appropriate for your finances, you will drastically improve your chances of reducing the frequency and the size of your losses.

Yes, I have bad days, but I can enjoy myself every day, secure in the knowledge that I am still in control and the bad times will not dull my humor nor devastate my pocketbook.

We all dream of winning the lottery or writing a bestseller that makes millions. Dreams inspire the world to greater deeds. They were the fuel that sent astronauts into orbit, encouraged them to land on the moon, and fired our space probes into the far reaches of the galaxy.

Well, dreams come back to earth quickly, and they crash hard in the harsh environment of the casino; the loftier the dream, the more certain and calamitous the crash.

I respect the dreamers of the world. My friends tell me I am one of them, but I cast my dreams aside long before I reach the casino door. Once there, I step carefully around the litter of other people's lofty expectations.

Casinos promise wealth in abundance; they deliver little. For every person they make rich, they take from a throng of others. Yes, there are millions in casinos—millions of losers.

I have met many slot players. I met a rare one only a few weeks before finishing the first draft of this book—I was sitting close by when he won $100,000 in a tournament. I have met other winners, too, but I am yet to meet a millionaire who made his millions from slot machines.

Most of the people I meet are the same as you and I, ordinary people out to have fun, recoup their costs for the day, and make a few dollars. Their aspirations are modest.

But there are the others, those constantly in search of that huge win they hope will set them up for life—the win that never comes. The only huge thing on their horizon is the debt they have incurred searching for the impossible. There is better chance of Big Foot being discovered browsing the Seattle suburbs than of these players fulfilling their dream.

So what is realistic for a winning day at the slots?

Think of your profit goal not as a pie-in-the-sky lump sum which bears little relation to the money you risk, but as a businessman would, a percentage return on your investment.

Since playing slot machines intelligently might involve as much preparation as some occupations without assurance of any return, it may be somewhat inaccurate to call your wager an investment. Yet there is a relationship between the amount of money you put into the machines and what you take out. Unlike buying bonds, however, where the more you invest the more you earn, there is a point of diminishing returns in slots when profit potential decreases dramatically.

Remember the exercise in chapter 4 to show the effects of repeated exposure to the casino hold? The trick is to balance time and money, to buy those Windows of Opportunity but to stay within their limits at each session.

You should be fully funded for the strategy you are working but it is foolhardy to risk too much money. The more you bring with you, the more you are likely to spend and the more you will probably lose, which would undermine our goals—more fun and fewer losses.

My win goal, depending on the strategy I am using and the level of risk I am prepared to accept, varies between 15 percent and 25 percent of my daily stake.

In the Green Plan, which emphasizes protection, I sacrifice some of the win potential inherent in other strategies, but I have found it difficult to lose using that system. So, in return for keeping most of my stake intact, I expect less profit. We can't have it all ways.

The other work plans are more aggressive, but I suggest you

use the guidelines in the protocol for each of them when determining your win goals.

That way, you will dramatically improve the prospect of enjoying your days at the slot machines and you will not feel cheated if the best you can do in the win column is $150 or $200.

When you have realistic expectations, you will be satisfied when everything goes right. Should you strike big, you will be as exultant as I am when I make $500 or $1,000 profit for the day or for the trip.

I mentioned the man who won $100,000 at a slot tournament. I was also participating and won money, but not enough to cover my entry fee.

For readers with limited budgets they are ready to write off as a fair cost for their holiday entertainment, slot tournaments are worth serious consideration. You might make money but, win or lose, you will enjoy the experience.

Most tournaments are staged over two or three days, though actual playing time is probably only one to two hours each day. Sponsoring casinos produce their schedules well ahead of time which will enable you to plan your trip and set aside the money you need.

The entry fee depends on the prize amounts. An average fee for a tournament with one or more $30,000 to $50,000 prizes is between $500 and $700, roughly equivalent to the bankroll for a single day's play on dollar slots. That fee is less than it seems because most times it includes accommodation, meals, drinks, and a dinner show.

Participants are limited in number, usually between four hundred and six hundred. The prizes are guaranteed and a high percentage of players will get at least some of their money back on one of the days, maybe $100 or $200.

You probably have to finish in the Top Ten one day to cover the entry fee but with daily or overall prizes in the tens of thousands, or even hundreds of thousands of dollars, the lucky people who strike the right slots can reap big money rewards.

Note the word *lucky*. In tournaments, you draw for your participant number and you draw for the machines you play. All the hints I can give you for daily use on stand-alone slot machines do not apply to tournaments. It is luck, pure and simple.

My luck has not been great at tournaments, but I have won money on five of the last seven days I have played. Twice I have come close to getting the entry fee back and, yes, I have won money regularly in free tournaments. I don't accept all invitations but over the past two years I have timed several trips to Las Vegas to coincide with tournaments for three reasons: complimentary meals, accommodations, etc; the chance of winning more money than I could from regular play; and the certainty that, because tournament participants are keen slot machine players, there will be enough activity at my target slots to improve the prospects of making money.

I prosper more when there is a high level of activity in the casino. People at tournaments are more likely to know which machines to play because they are more experienced. They may not know the best way to play these machines but they do know where to play.

That brings another bonus for me. There are more people to observe at tournament time, more opportunities to add to my knowledge.

Talk about winning all ways!

9

What Casino?
Which Slots?

So you have the right mental approach and have allocated the amount of money you can afford to risk. The next critical decisions are where to put your Managed Luck into operation and which machines to play.

Make the wrong selections and your winning goals will become much more difficult to achieve.

I liken these decisions to the choices facing one on the beach. Loiter on a down slope from a rising tide, sooner or later you are going to get wet; stay on higher ground, you will be safe.

Slot machines, too, can give you a soaking if you start out in the wrong place and linger there too long.

THE RIGHT CASINO

I use several measures to rate casinos; the five most important to me, not necessarily in order, are:

- comfort
- accessibility
- availability of target machines

- payout features
- payback percentages

As concentration is an essential part of my strategies, I always dress casually and choose comfortable surroundings. I try to avoid casinos where the noise level is too high or the slots area too congested.

Since my ideals of silence and solitude will not be found in any casino, I have to compromise, but even in the most popular establishments, there are times (early morning, mid-afternoon, early evening, or after midnight) when there are fewer people and action on the casino floor is more subdued.

I'm happiest where smoking is prohibited but a prudent choice of hour usually allows me to avoid this irritant in most places.

Since the Riviera and Westward Ho market to older people and retirees, these casinos are quieter no matter how large the crowd—and both places are often crowded, especially on weekends and holidays.

Big crowds do not necessarily translate into restricted access to target machines. I may have to wait longer for the chance to play the right machines, but I don't object to this since, on balance, the more activity in a casino the greater my prospects of doing well. The pauses also give me a chance to regroup and observe what is happening around me.

Assuming I can get to the machines I want without much delay, the biggest drawback is distraction when the aisles are jammed and everyone is chattering incessantly.

Many casinos subscribe to the theory that the rowdier the place, the more exciting the atmosphere. Judging by the throngs at Primadonna on the California state line and bigger casinos such as Circus Circus and Excalibur, they may be right, but constant cacophony does not suit me. I have found I prosper in a more peaceful atmosphere.

It stands to reason that the temperature within the casino

should be comfortable. After all, you will be there a while.

Dark casinos may suit those who prefer dark restaurants and bars, but I like a bright, airy place with plenty of walk space for people to move along the aisles without stepping over the players. I look for comfortable stools so I can sit at the machines rather than stand. A pet grievance of mine is finding only two or three stools to ten machines or a full carousel. I could name several casinos where the aisles between machines are cramped so tightly it is sometimes impossible to move freely from one place to another. Perhaps because of this lack of space, there are not enough stools for patrons in these places even at the slowest times.

Common sense tells us, as each slot machine is a separate source of revenue for the casino, the more slots in a given area, the more people can be playing at the same time, and the more money the casino will make.

I believe the layout of the casino floor speaks volumes about the attitude of any casino enterprise to its customers. Casinos which cram as many slots as possible onto their floors are showing scant respect for the comfort and welfare of their patrons; their business philosophy is simple—extract maximum profit from each square foot of space.

These same places are more likely to hustle hard in other ways. I remember one, in a state which legislates the minimum payout at 80 percent, where it was virtually impossible for two people to pass in the aisles between the rows of slots. I doubt they could have packed more machines into that place had they been piled atop each other.

I don't think it coincidental that the casino win in that location seemed extraordinarily high, i.e., the odds were really stacked against the players there.

Not only were the chances of winning reduced but other customer services were expensive or conspicuously absent. Snack bar prices were high, the restaurant had little to recommend it, I did not see a drinks hostess anywhere, and a bottle of beer at the bar cost as much as it would at an airport.

At that time, there was little or no competition within reasonable proximity. The situation may have improved since my visit as several casinos are now plying their trade in the area.

A casino which cares about its patrons will consider their comfort. There will be room to move around, the slots will be spaced to give players plenty of elbow room, most machines will have seats or stools, and the layout will project a sense of welcome and respectability. A friendly ambience and adequate facilities should add up to more enjoyment.

Of course, you should look for a balance. I would be suspicious of any establishment with too few machines and too much free space. Simple business arithmetic tells us there must be a compromise between the profit interests of the casino and the comfort of its patrons.

Be as wary of wide open environs as you are of places packed tight with slots. Somebody has to pay for the wasted space. That somebody may be you by way of a higher win for the casino from each dollar you spend there. Profits are the lifeblood of all prosperous businesses and only the more successful gaming establishments can afford to continue to give their customers the best odds and creature comforts.

All these elements are part of the total atmosphere in the casino and are intrinsic to your choice of where to play. There is, however, one other aspect which can override almost everything I have mentioned so far.

I call this the Casino Handshake.

Any reader who has been to Westward Ho on the Las Vegas Strip will know precisely what I mean. Management policy is clearly to make slot players feel at home. From the moment out-of-towners check in at the registration desk or casual visitors walk through the front door, they are part of the casino family.

The staff makes a point of being friendly. Carousel attendants are quick to introduce themselves and offer help. Even though the cynics among us know this attitude is not spontaneous and altruistic but is dictated by policy, it is refreshing when employees offer straight answers to customer questions. Westward Ho employees seem to have a genuine interest in customers as individuals rather than merely as mobile tokens whose money pays their wages.

Compare this friendly reception with the indifference at many other places where casino staff are too preoccupied or busy to answer questions. Some seem so poorly trained they couldn't give you information even were they inclined to do so.

I am sure all regulars have encountered change booth operators who shut the window when they see you coming and hostesses who never appear to take your drink order or take it but do not return.

The Casino Handshake is important to me; it should also be important to casino management because it works.

In the course of my research for this book, I interviewed a number of casino executives and invited them to complete questionnaires.

One question concerned frequency of visits. The average repeat frequency reported by Westward Ho is significantly higher than all other casinos answering my questionnaire and is well above the overall average for gambling visitors to Nevada. Not surprising, the next best was the Riviera.

No accident. To a greater or lesser extent, the Casino Handshake is strongly evident in each of these casinos because they go out of their way to welcome customers, attend to their needs, and give all comers the same chance of winning.

There are many casinos which place a high priority on customer relations. I suggest you look for them. If we demand more comfort and better treatment from all casinos, they will respond.

After all, gaming is a competitive business and only the best will thrive.

I discussed comfort and atmosphere first because these factors are important to the environment in which you will be working.

Some readers may think my priorities are wrong—that accessibility to a casino is more important than what may be offered inside. Who cares if a casino has everything going for it when it is two thousand miles away and there is a new riverboat within a ten-minute drive? Simple logic says most people will opt for the riverboat.

That is probably true but then most people don t win money at slots and don't bother making these choices iet alone explore their options before they make strategy decisions.

I am not against riverboats though I have some concern about the potential social impact in many of the areas they are located or planned.

What suits one reader may not work for another. I have visited several riverboats. Like casinos in Las Vegas and Atlantic City or on American Indian reservations, some provide an environment where I know I should fare well. Others do not. That should not mean these places won't suit you.

Casinos which rely mostly on local custom may not be as stable long term as those which draw a high percentage of their customers from a wider area.

Convenience gambling establishments, as these are called, feed on local communities. Specialty houses in destination resorts not only derive most of their revenue from more distant sources because of their wider geographical draw, but also create business for other services such as airlines, taxis, buses, hotels, motels, restaurants, and other stores. Convenience casinos are more likely to divert funds from local businesses, to the detriment of the whole community.

Proximity can lead to many of the problems opponents of gambling predict and may prove to be a deadly trap for the unwary, the undisciplined, or the poorly financed. The statement is worth repeating: A casino which is too easy to access may too often lure you into unplanned visits. Spontaneity is a wonderful quality but don't let yourself be seduced into running down the road to the next casino before you are fully prepared and adequately financed to make that visit.

The temptation to try and win back what you lost last night can be very hard to withstand when there is a casino within easy driving distance.

On the other hand, if you have to budget airfare for an out-of-state destination, you are more likely to finance the trip adequately and do the homework, which will better prepare you to manage your luck.

THE RIGHT SLOT MACHINES

Ideal casino surroundings are of little value if you cannot get access to the right slots. The best system in the world will not work unless there are enough target machines and you can reach them without too much trouble.

In the next chapter, we describe the various types of slot machines. While many look similar from the outside, they can be quite different. It is important that you familiarize yourself with the configurations well enough to recognize which is which, to know what the variations mean, and to gauge their likely impact on your success or failure. Only in this way will you be able to make prudent decisions about which machines to play and which to avoid.

Your choice of target machine may be different from mine, but whatever you decide, I strongly recommend you restrict your sessions to the same type and denomination. Move around but do not switch around. There is a critical distinction.

For a slots circuit to have any real chance of generating winning results consistently, there must be at least six readily accessible target slots to support twelve machine sessions in a day and no fewer than eight for a fifteen session day.

On my main circuit in Las Vegas, each location offers more

than the minimum number of my target machines. That means I am able to complete a full machine roster at one place or I have a broader selection when one casino is crowded and machine access could otherwise become a problem.

While payback percentages are important, so are the payout features of the machines. By payout features, I am referring to the hit frequency of the target machines, their pay tables or header boards, and their capacity to store credits during play.

As strange as it may seem, I know of at least one major casino in Las Vegas which has all its machines set to spill out each return, big or small, immediately. It is impossible to accumulate session credits in any of their slots. Management must work on the theory that the continuous din will make people think there are more winners and encourage them to linger longer.

My reaction is the opposite. The constant noise affects my concentration. More significant, if I am unable to store accumulating credits while a machine session is in progress, I am deprived of an essential element in my money management strategies. Accordingly, I will not patronize casinos with instant payouts no matter how many of my target machines they have on-line.

I recommend the same caveat to you—no accumulations, no patronage. You will dramatically improve your prospects of winning with this one decision because, simply put, if you cannot control your money, you cannot control your slot machine sessions or your working day.

Readers may be unfamiliar with the terms hits, payout frequency, and pay tables or, as they are sometimes called, pay boards or header boards. Learn to recognize these terms and know what they mean.

Our prospects of winning will be boosted considerably when we learn to identify machines with favorable payout frequencies and pay boards and make it a policy to avoid those which do not meet our criteria.

Fortunately, we can learn what we need to know fairly quickly from the pay tables on the slot machines and from closely observing other people before we play ourselves. We can then test our conclusions during our own sessions.

Let me give you an example. My target slots are IGT Red, White, and Blue. These machines are popular everywhere, ranking number one in the nation in a recent survey. In fact, IGT machines filled nine of the top ten revenue-earning slot machines in the nation last year. That means more people play Red, White, and Blues than any other machine. It follows that most casinos will have several. Some establishments have whole rows or carousels.

Why then do I restrict my efforts on these machines to only a few places? First, I am not interested in *all* Red, White, and Blue machines. They may look alike but they are not all alike.

Although I have won an all-coins-in jackpot on a three coin machine with a ten thousand coin payoff, I rarely play that type of slot now except when I am experimenting or trying to validate a change in working strategy.

I narrow my interest to two coiners and I prefer those with a single pay line and a maximum one thousand coin top line payout. This latter choice flies in the face of popular habit. Machines with five thousand or ten thousand coin top lines attract far more customers than those offering one thousand coin top line returns. Lured by the size of the possible jackpot, the average casino customer does not realize the chances of hitting any jackpot diminish at least in reverse proportion to the increase in the size of the payout.

Information from a reliable source indicates that another popular IGT slot, the Double Diamond three coin machine with two thousand five hundred coin top line, is likely to hit that payout eight times more frequently than the same game program which offers a ten thousand coin jackpot. If this is true,

which machine do you think you would be better off playing?
Now, guess which machine most casino goers will play!

However, since top line payouts are few and far between
and most casino patrons will grow old without hitting a single
jackpot, it is the overall strength in the remainder of the pay
board which really counts for me.

A slot with a 97 percent payback will return 97 percent of
the money it takes in over a given number of pay cycles no
matter what. That means you should logically expect a better
chance of winning from the core of the pay table and the pay
frequency on a 97 percent machine with a one thousand coin
top line than on the same payback percentage machine with a
five thousand or ten thousand coin jackpot. My experiences
tend to confirm that theory.

Although some casinos may still have more three coin
machines, the trend today seems to be towards two coiners,
especially in the dollar denomination. Slot managers noticed
patrons in 1994 and 1995 were more likely to risk maximum play
on two coin rather than three coin machines.

So what is the difference between a Red, White, and Blue
two coiner at one location and a Red, White, and Blue two
coiner with an identical pay table at another? Why do I seem to
do much better in one place than the other?

PAYOUT FREQUENCY

The answer could lie in the frequency of payouts, i.e., the
average number of hits or payouts over one hundred, two
hundred, or three hundred spins. As strange as it may seem, a
machine can hit too often, especially one like the Red, White,
and Blue which pays out on as many as fifteen different symbol
combinations, including blanks. Lots of little hits can mean
insufficient bigger wins to allow a fair chance of making money.

The pay frequency on slots, which look the same in all

discernible ways, may well be different, just as the payback percentages can differ. Since you can't be certain of these variables, unless the casino posts the details (and few do), you are somewhat at the mercy of the house which is another reason some casinos offer a more favorable winning environment than others. It is not always the fault of management. You won't find payback percentages posted anywhere in Atlantic City because the state gaming authority will not permit such displays.

Pay frequency and payback percentages are determined by casino policy. They originate with the machine order. One casino may ask for the highest pay frequency and the highest payback available for the game program it wants; another may give the machine manufacturer a list of specifications to meet or opt for a less generous version of the same program.

I do not begrudge the hours I spend watching other people play slots. This is truly valuable time because only by watching what is happening when others are at my target machines can I get any sort of line on pay frequencies and payback percentages.

I try to be as unobtrusive as possible when I do this. Some people are uneasy when they realize they are being watched. I overcome this in two ways. I may politely ask players if they mind my watching for a while or I may switch positions and appear to be more interested in other slots. My goal at these moments is not to see if the player is having a losing or winning streak. I long ago came to the conclusion that, on the modern computerized slot, there may be short-term winning patterns but there is little value to be gained in seeking machines which appear to be hot or those which seem overdue for a big win. I would have to watch through many entire pay cycles to make those deductions and I doubt whether I would gain anything from the knowledge.

What I am looking for is some measure of the pay frequency and the payback percentage. The figures I come up with cannot be 100 percent accurate but will be fairly reliable guides.

My idea of pay frequency will differ markedly from both the casino order and the manufacturer's specification. The reason is that we tally the frequency differently.

For the casino and the manufacturer, hits include Coins Back and Double Coins Back. For example, blanks on all three reels may return your coins for that spin while cherries may bring two for one. To me, neither is worth factoring in and I ignore them in my calculation of payout frequencies.

On most machines, the bulk of the payouts may be window dressing. At the end of the day, they mean little. I have yet to find a slot player who prefers a series of coins back to a set of double or treble bars.

Accordingly, when a casino rates a machine as having a payout frequency of one in 5.4 or one in 6.7, it is saying that slot will average one payout in either 5.4 spins or 6.7 spins. The 5.4 machine could be considered loose in most casinos while the 6.7 may be a little tighter than average but neither means the hits will come on a regular cycle to match that frequency. That doesn't happen. Payouts come in batches and there can be long periods between hits.

As far as I am concerned, the calculation that matters is the number of worthwhile payouts. This is the figure I look for when I check out a slot machine. I disregard those small hits. On slots with pay frequencies of one in 5.4, one in 6.3, one in 6.5, or whatever, the hits that make a real contribution toward a profit are more likely to occur at one in 12, one in 18 or even as few as one in 25.

Since the casino isn't going to give me this information, I must seek it out myself. My minimum criteria are payouts which return more than double coins. I disregard any return under four coins back for each coin played on that spin.

How can I get this figure? Clicking a simple handheld tally counter or doing some mental addition as I observe other players will give me an answer. I will watch play at what I consider a likely machine through several 100 to 200 spin cycles at peak times and arrive at an average number of hits over a given number of spins.

Because of the natural or chance fluctuation in hits, the longer the evaluation period the more accurate the calculation. This is why this task is best achieved when there are plenty of people in the casino who are staying long enough at each slot to generate meaningful figures.

If the average over a total of three hundred to five hundred spins is in the region of twelve or more qualifying payouts per one hundred spins, it is probably too high to offer a fair chance of profit. Too much of the payback percentage is consumed in smaller payouts. Remember, these are in addition to the hits that, in my evaluation, don't count.

Let's take an example. We will assume in theory what is almost impossible in practice—an exact return from one hundred spins on a slot with 95 percent payback. For simplicity, we will say the investment is one coin per spin. So we have $95 coming back. Assume this machine has a payout frequency of one to 6.3, then we can expect our $95 will come from sixteen hits. If twelve of these are qualifying and four are money back, the return on the qualifying payouts will be $95 − $4 = $91. Over twelve hits, that is an average of $7.58. We may have a fair chance of getting most of our money back but little prospect of winning.

Should our calculations indicate as few as four or five qualifying payouts per one hundred spins, then there may be too many money-back hits for comfort and insufficient qualifiers for a reasonable chance of one larger payout. I may elect to run additional checks in this situation but will probably move on to more fertile fields.

I become intrigued when the count is between six and nine per one hundred spins. My experience is best results will come on machines with payouts in that range.

Why is this? In the chapter entitled "The Fundamentals of Winning," I said I expect to have an overall average of two small or losing payouts for each win which covers the investment over the previous ten spins and leaves me with a profit.

In other words, we need those six to nine qualifying hits per one hundred spins to have a mathematical chance of hitting that bigger payout. Since we are unlikely to stay at the same slot for one hundred spins, the potential number of qualifying hits will be reduced to three to five per session. One of those could be big enough to return a profit for the session or perhaps for the whole day.

PAYBACK PERCENTAGES

Unfortunately it is much harder to get an accurate gauge of the actual payback percentages. All the vigilance and concentration in the world cannot guarantee that you will be able to pick the right slot on an "Up to 97.4 percent" carousel.

My recommendation is simple. When you have selected your target machines, play them in popular casinos which have plenty of healthy competition from other locations in close proximity. Inside the chosen casinos, stick to areas where the highest paybacks are posted. In all probability, you will have a better chance of winning there than at other locations in those casinos.

There is a negative measure which may help but, to be of any value, it will be costly and it runs counter to my machine allocations anyway.

On a machine with a payback of 97 percent, in normal play you can expect to lose $100 in two hours at an average five spins per minute with three coins in; you could lose the same amount of money in only one hour on a 94 percent payback slot.

PAY BOARDS

We have already discussed my preference for slots with lower top line jackpots and I have talked about the importance of selecting machines with strong payboards overall rather than those elusive big top line lures.

Pay boards. Pay tables. Header boards. Call them what you will, they provide information every slot player should have and understand before he or she inserts that first coin.

It is folly to walk up to any machine, put in your money and, when the reels stop spinning, look up to see what you should get from the symbols combination showing. Yet people frequently do this, then they wonder why the set of red sevens isn't paying out when the header board has one hundred coins listed against that combination. More often than not, they become furious with the machine and feel they have been hoodwinked out of their due.

Unfortunately, this scenario is repeated every day. It is not the fault of the slot or the management. Players have nobody to blame but themselves if they let this happen.

The example given here is the most elementary. The player has assumed that all symbol combinations showing on the header board will pay out, irrespective of coins played.

On a multiplier, this is correct. But the slot will not pay a solitary cent if it is an Option-Buy—a machine where extra coins are needed to buy all winning combinations and the player has failed to play the number of coins required to activate the combination showing in the glass.

The Universal Company's Magnificent Sevens is a favorite. These machines, known by a variety of names, are the automatic choice of tournament operators everywhere and receive a tremendous amount of nontournament play.

In the past few years, Magnificent Sevens has been the only slot to break IGT brand dominance of the ten best money earners, ranking sixth in the nation for 1993 and 1994. In earlier years, it was ranked higher.

Although two coins buy a proportionate increase in payouts for all blank or bar combinations on Magnificent Sevens, the machines are not true multipliers. To activate any Sevens combination, you must play three coins.

Mixed sevens, red sevens, blue sevens mean nothing unless

you have played the third coin on each spin. As these are the big payoff combinations (except for three bars with two coins in), it is a blow for many players when they hit Magnificent Sevens and end up with nothing.

Compared to many other slots, the pay table is clear and concise. There is no excuse for not reading and understanding what it shows.

The same cannot be said for some other option-buy machines which require extra coins to activate bigger payout combinations. It can be difficult to decipher their busy header boards.

Each additional coin played on these slots buys colorful symbols which look much the same until you study them closely. For example, you will see the clown symbol is just a little different from the double jackpot, the triple jackpot, or the home run. Because the bar portions of the winning combinations are often the same for each coin played and the option-buy symbols are so similar in appearance, even experienced players can fall into the same trap.

The rule is Player Beware. Unless you are prepared to risk maximum coins each spin, you should avoid option buy machines. I keep to true multipliers simply because of my controlled investments, the loss limits I have set, and the protocols I follow in the casino. The strategies, systems, and work plans I use are predicated on restricting my activities to multiplier machines.

What do I mean by strength in the pay board?

When I study header boards, I am not looking for any particular number of payout combinations. Some machines offer six pay combinations per coin, others eight or nine; Red, White, and Blues have fifteen and Black Gold slots seventeen.

Clearly, a machine with fifteen or seventeen pay lines is going to offer more small hits than the machine with only six or eight, but that does not mean there is any great advantage in playing one machine rather than the other.

The yardstick that matters is the proportion of payouts above 50 percent of the total number of coins I will allocate to that machine should I decide to play it.

On Red, White, and Blue regular machines, there are eight such combinations of fifteen total. The wild card version of that same slot has nine of eighteen. The Double Diamond may have only seven winning combinations but four of them fall into this higher payout category, and the doubling feature of this machine brings a fifth bigger payout possibility into play—single bars.

When any single hit during a session returns 50 percent or more of the money at risk, I can be confident I will win money at that session or at least get most of my investment back.

Though I discount token coins back in the analysis of the pay frequencies which count, naturally I welcome their contributions when I am actually at the machines. Several of these small hits, plus one or two 50 percent or better returns, and I am well on my way to making a profit on that session.

So be sure to scrutinize those pay boards. There may be a lot of information to digest on some slots, less on others, but you need to understand everything those headers tell you before you sit down to work or play. This is part of your preparation and there can be no substitute.

Does this apply to all slot machines?

The answer is yes. Even though all machines with the same payout percentage will, over a period of several pay cycles, pay out the same amount of money given the same volume of play, what really counts is the way in which that money is paid out.

I have one last comment before we look at the various types of machines in the next chapter.

Slots can be found virtually everywhere in Nevada: airports, supermarkets, bus terminals, drug stores, bars, and restaurants.

These locations are traps for the unwary.

If you really intend to manage your luck wisely and enhance your winning prospects, even if you see several of your target slots in those places, walk right by. Do not stop! Do not be tempted! Do not spend a single dollar there!

♠ **Stay with machines which get continuous play in the most competitive environments seven days a week, fifty-two weeks a year.**

The supermarket knows the proportion of its customers who will spend all their change on the slots. It doesn't have to compete with casinos on payout frequencies or payback percentages and it doesn't care about player retention. The average customer stays only until the change is gone just as the airport player will leave on hearing the boarding call.

The bar patron can be relied on to play slots or video poker machines no matter how poor the prospects of winning. The couple waiting for a table at the restaurant or a plane at the airport or a bus at the downtown terminal do not expect to win; they are merely filling time.

There is no valid reason these places should offer the best odds. Take it from me, they do not. In states which set minimum lower limits for payback percentages—83 percent in New Jersey, 80 percent in several others—you can rest assured where slots are permitted in locations other than casinos, they are unlikely to pay more than the minimum. In Nevada, where there is now a 75 percent lower limit on payback percentages per machine or location average, the return can be even worse. Theoretically, it could be 75 percent or less.

In contrast, casinos which compete fiercely for lodging and visitor business must stay highly competitive in every way if they are to succeed in keeping visitors away from other establishments. Even more competitive are casinos which target sophisticated, experienced local slots players. Downtown Las Vegas is such a place.

This is reflected in the financial reports from the state gaming control board. While we know there can be significant differences between payback percentages at casinos in any given area and among nickel, quarter, and dollar machines within each casino, group figures can tell us a lot.

When the overall average slots win for casinos on The Strip hovers around 4.4 percent, is 4.2 percent in downtown Las Vegas, is more likely to be 8 percent or 9 percent in most other places, and can reach 12 percent, 15 percent, or more at individual slot circuit locations, it is obvious where we should risk our dollars.

Concentrate on the right machines in the right locations. Things can still go wrong but at least you dramatically reduce the odds against winning and will give yourself a reasonable chance for more break-even or profitable days.

10

Beware of Wolves in Sheep's Clothing: Look-Alikes are Not All Alike

It's time to examine the various types of machines and find out what we mean when we talk about multipliers, single pay lines, progressive slots, or three line option-buys.

I have deliberately left this section until late in the book. My emphasis so far has been on the elements in human behavior I am convinced have as much or more influence than software and hardware on whether we win or lose.

By first learning the fundamentals of winning, as outlined in the acronym PLAN WORK, we have established a solid base for our evaluation of the variations among machines and for recognizing the significance of these differences.

First, some general observations.

While many people still refer to slots as one-armed bandits and manufacturers continue to produce machines with pull levers, few players tug those handles nowadays. It is a rare slot which does not offer a push button feature as an alternative method of spinning the reels.

Those handles are still the source of a lot of fanciful conjecture. Even today, in the era of computerized slots, some players cling to the idea that they can somehow control the spin mechanism by manipulation of the handle. They are sure that, with a slow or a fast pull or several breaks in the action (the pause-and-pull syndrome), they will boost their chances of hitting big.

The truth is they are doing nothing. Apart from activating the machine, handle pull techniques have no effect on the spinning or the symbols that show when the reels stop. In fact, much like scoreboards at basketball and football games, the reel strips on the modern slot function are simply electronic notice boards which show the winning or, more often, the losing result of each spin.

The factors that have an impact are the game program, the computer chips which control the action, and the Random Number Generator, or RNG, which works nonstop day and night, irrespective of whether anybody is playing the machine, to come up with a new number value for each millisecond of the day, the week, and the year. None of these devices can be controlled by any external force.

For all practical purposes, it is better to forsake the handle altogether. Consider it nothing more than an unnecessary appendage stuck on to the modern slot in the interest of tradition.

Not only is it easier and less tiring over time to press a button rather than tug on a handle, but it is a prudent safeguard against a frequently recurring and annoying problem manufacturers have not been able to overcome satisfactorily—the failure of slot machines to accept all coins played.

Somewhere on each slot you will find the statement "pays only on coins accepted." As each coin is inserted, a pay line or a section of the pay board will light up to signify what has been activated and the Coins Played meter will register the transaction.

It is not enough to insert your coins and pull the handle or press the button. The onus is upon you to be vigilant at all times, to check that the machine actually accepts your play.

You will get no sympathy from management when you complain about being shortchanged after hitting three sevens, triple bars, or any winning combination with three coins in, if the Coins Played meter has registered only two coins in play— or worse, just one.

The responsibility for the machine failure is yours. You must make the correction before you pull that handle or push that button. The situation cannot be remedied afterward. Lest you think this does not happen often, think again.

The life of a popular slot in a busy casino can be as little as two years. During that time, though the functions of the apparatus are controlled by computer, there is a tremendous amount of physical wear, tear, and abuse on the coin acceptors and payout mechanisms.

A three coin dollar machine played a mean of 2.1 coins in for an average of eight hours a day, seven days a week, over two years, will handle around $4.5 million over a two-year period. Every one of those dollar slugs must be physically taken into the machine, accepted, stored, and given out, either in payment on win combinations or in the casino drop, i.e., what is taken out of the machine in bulk on a daily basis.

Imagine the wear that must take place on the coin track over that cycle of four or five million transactions; then add to this equation the fact that all those coins or slugs are being constantly recycled and are themselves subject to rigorous wear and tear. How often do slugs fall straight through the machines? Hundreds of times each day.

No wonder slot machines too often fail to register all coins inserted and malfunction more than occasionally in other ways.

If the slot takes a coin but does not register the transaction and fails to return the coin, call an attendant so the problem can be corrected before you continue. It will be too late after the event, and winning combinations are hard enough to hit anyway without risking any portion of the payout through carelessness.

I mentioned earlier that using a button rather than the handle can be a safeguard. How? Slot machines have several buttons, each with a different function. These buttons light up when activated. You should know what they do and how to use them.

The button on the far left when you are facing the slot is the Change button on most machines. If you need more slugs or the machine jams, runs out of money without completing a full payout, or malfunctions some other way, press this button; a light will go on atop the slot and sooner or later an attendant will arrive to correct the problem.

The next button in from the left is the Cash or Credit button, an important device in any slots strategy. When you are ready to play, this is the button you press to tell the machine you want to accumulate the payouts. Press it again when you are ready to take your money out at the end of the session.

Since this is a money button, I strongly recommend you make a practice of pressing it several times before you leave the machine.

The middle button is generally marked Bet One Coin. If you follow my guidelines, you will use this button a lot, often in conjunction with the Spin Reels button usually found second from the right. Press the Bet One Coin button once for each coin you want to play (unless you are playing maximum coins), then press the Spin Reels button.

The button at the extreme right is usually Play Maximum Coins. When this is activated, the machine requires maximum coins inserted or taken from stored credits. Only when it finds them from one source or the other will it proceed with the next spin.

This is the ultimate protection against player or machine error. Use this button intentionally or by accident, the result will be the same, maximum coins played, or no play at all if the machine cannot find the coins either in credit or inserted for that play. Using this button, it is impossible to finish with less money than is due from a winning symbols combination.

There are some situations where it is absolutely vital you use the Play Maximum Coins button to set the reels in motion. When playing progressive slots, especially wide-area progressive slots such as IGT's Nevada Nickels, Quartermania, or Megabucks, use the button for every play.

Because of the reduced odds and the percentage being taken out to fund the jackpot, the only rationale for playing WAPS machines is, in my opinion, the remote possibility of hitting one of those huge jackpots. That can be achieved only with maximum coins.

Forget the handle. Forget the Spin Reels button. When you intend to play maximum coins make it your practice to use Play Maximum Coins to start every spin.

There is a lot of information on the modern slot machine apart from the header or pay board details that I emphasized in an earlier chapter. All notices are important. Read and understand them. For example, Malfunction Voids All Plays and Pays.

This may not mean what you think. I have overheard people discussing the statement and been surprised at the number who misinterpret it. This is not a promise of payouts if and when the slot malfunctions. This tells you the play is voided and there will be no payout no matter what symbols show at the stop. Big difference!

As I mentioned in an earlier chapter, many newer slot machines have bill changers that enable players to feed notes into the machine instead of leaving to get more slugs or calling for change. Some changers take notes as small as $1 or as large as $100.

While these are useful and convenient features, they benefit the casino more than the player. With a full complement of bill changers on the floor, casinos profit big in two ways. First, they need fewer people to work the change carts, thus saving on equipment costs, salaries, and wages. Second, more patrons will stay at the machines for longer periods, which boosts revenues.

This is a classic example of what is good for the goose being far better for the gander. Take this casino consideration for convenience to the next stage and we have the ultimate feature, those credit-swipe devices we discussed earlier. They are already in use on international airlines which offer gambling as a diversion for passengers. Sooner or later, they will be coming to a casino near you.

I repeat—caution! The big winners will not be the players who make a habit of using these conveniences. You might as well set up automatic transfers direct from your bank or credit card accounts to the casinos.

No slot machine will pay out the full amount of a big hit, nor will it store more credits than the $1,200 win total which triggers an IRS filing. Because of this, you may run into situations which can cost money if you are not mindful.

In the event you strike a big payout when there were credits registered before the hit, these credits will still be there after you have been paid.

The slot will pay out only what the notice on the machine indicates. This may be as little as $400 or $600 on a dollar slot or as many as one thousand coins on a quarter machine. An attendant will pay the balance, usually in cash but you can ask for a check. Casinos call this a hand-paid win.

The attendant will not pay out what had already accrued on the credit meter before the win. You must cash that out.

People who believe they should leave the machine imme-diately after a hand-paid win will sometimes forget their credits.

Recently, I saw a woman start to walk away from a machine with more than $1,000 in cash, not realizing she was leaving $245 in credits accumulated before her big win. On that occasion, the attendant drew her attention to the oversight but it is unreasonable to expect that will happen every time. Attendants have other responsibilities and may not notice. And if the player at the next machine does not spot your credits—or isn't honest enough to tell you—it will be your loss and somebody else's gain.

The same situation can occur for midsize wins. Most slots pay hits of $400 or more immediately, even if you have the credit meter running. When this happens, the machine pays out only that single win. Credits already in the machine stay there.

Have you ever noticed people wandering around casinos studying slot meters and looking in the coin trays? They can make a tidy sum this way because customers leave credits in the machines or money in the trays dozens of times each day.

Unlike the nearby player who observes what is happening and says nothing, most times this is not a question of honesty. Who knows who left money in a machine when the last player has long gone?

You wouldn't expect a methodical and experienced player to make the mistake of leaving a machine with credits in the meter. Yet I have done so several times. I have written the results of a session in my little book, then walked away without the money. Now I make a habit of cashing out first, then doing my tallying.

Most times, I have quickly realized my oversight and retrieved the cash but, on at least two occasions, I recall arriving to find another player already at the machine. Luckily, little money was involved.

However, those small oversights can add up to far too much money to give away. If it happens after a winning payout, there may be a lot of cash involved. Fortunately, most of us are more attentive when there is big money to collect and rarely leave more than a few coins.

I have also benefitted from the oversight of other players. It is a rare visit, especially in the early morning, when I do not find some coins in a tray or a credit on a meter. On balance, I have probably picked up more than I have left.

Some slots have strange looking symbols or feature different devices to attract players.

The most common are wild card and double payout symbols. The wild cards are substitutes for other symbols and can make the difference between a winning and a losing payout.

If the other symbols are part of a possible payout lineup then the wild card will complete the combination.

Double payout symbols are a combination of a wild card and a multiplication feature. When one of these finishes on the payline not only can it turn the stop into a winning combination, but it will double the payout. Complete a winning combination with two double symbols and the payout will be four times what is showing on the header board.

The Nudge feature is beginning to appear more frequently on new machines. This is not a recent innovation. Nudge machines were prevalent in England and Europe years ago. Some people fancy them because they are a little different. If the Nudge symbol stops above or below the payline, and the arrow (or rocket, gun, or plane) is pointed toward the line, the symbol will move to the pay line and may complete a pay combination.

Other intriguing devices include Spin till Payout and Repeat the Win. Both do precisely what they promise. Get a Spin till Win symbol on the line, and the reels will kick off spontaneously and keep spinning until they hit a winning combination. Some Repeat the Win machines keep players guessing because they never know just when the feature will choose to repeat a payout.

The previous general comments apply to all types of slots. Now I'll discuss the specifics—the important differences in machines.

DENOMINATIONS

Would you believe you can play slots with as little as one cent or as much as $500 invested on a single play?

Though one cent slots are difficult to find, these little guys are alive and well in some casinos. Collectively they attract more than $1 million in play each month in Nevada alone. That adds up to more than one hundred million pennies tumbling around.

At the end of the first quarter of 1994, there were 169 one cent slot machines in Nevada. Of these, 144 were in Clark County, which includes Las Vegas and Laughlin. Most are at the Gold Spike, the Western Hotel, and Union Plaza but a few can be found at Silver City and Little Caesar's Casino.

At the far end of affordability are the $100 and $500 machines. There are ninety-one $100 machines and nineteen $500 machines in Nevada alone. You can also find them in Atlantic City.

The $100 machines are fairly well spread through the high-roller havens and some of the less grandiose spots on the Strip but, if you want to experience the vicarious pleasure of watching some deep-pocketed sport lose $500 on a single spin, you will have to go to Caesar's Palace or Caesar's Tahoe, Harrah's Tahoe, the MGM Grand, the Mirage, or the Las Vegas Hilton.

For the average player, playing any of these big ticket machines, even $5 and $25 denominations, would be fiscal suicide. Unless your budget runs into the tens of thousands and your common sense is less common than most, my recommendation is to let them be.

The average casino win on these mammoths may be less than 1 percent overall on the $100 and $500 machines and less than 2 percent on the $25 units but the downside is that even these percentages can slaughter most players.

Small as the entry fee may be, one cent machines are no bargain either. The overall casino win exceeds 10 percent even in downtown Las Vegas and on the Strip. Although you are unlikely to do a great deal of damage to the family budget at a few cents a spin, the trade-off is that there is precious little prospect of making money.

By far the most popular slots are the nickel, quarter, and dollar machines.

Readers may be surprised to know that, in many casinos, nickel machines get almost as much play as quarter slots. Casino managers may be loathe to admit it but they love their nickel slots. Their win may not add up to as many dollars overall as the large denomination machines but that important percentage, at an average of 9 percent or 10 percent or more is probably at least double that of even the tightest quarter or dollar areas on their slot floors.

One astute executive in Las Vegas has shown me his arithmetic which proves that, for the same square footage and lower personnel costs, he can make more money from a bay of nickel slots than from his blackjack pit. Is it then any wonder casino managers can't hide smiles when they see their nickel slot areas crowded to capacity?

The comparatively low payback percentage is the reason I avoid nickels, but even I admit playing them can be fun, an appropriate stake is much less than required for quarter or dollar machines, and even on bad days, most patrons will be able to keep their losses within budget.

There are plenty of dime slots around and recently I have

noticed more fifty cent machines. Dime machines seem to get relatively little play and their win percentage is too low to interest me.

Fifty cent slots are a different matter. As you would expect, the average casino win overall is lower on these for quarter machines and compares well with dollar slots. In fact, at the larger, more competitive casinos in downtown Las Vegas, the payback (at more than 97 percent average) is higher than for *any* machine other than those big-ticket dreammakers.

This suggests to me that, if you can find a casino which has a sufficient number of your target slots in the 50 cent denominations, it could be worth working some of your daily sessions around them.

In theory with all other things being equal, the win potential should be there, especially as the daily stake requirement to conduct the recommended work plans will be around $300, half what is required for the dollar machines.

However, all things may not be equal. Although there are more fifty cent machines around now, I have no experience trying them. First, there are too few of my target slots in fifty cent machines in the casinos I patronize to sustain a full daily program. Second, even in places that do have enough machines, such as Harrah's and Palace Station, my observations indicate the volume of play is still quite small and that translates into fewer winning opportunities.

I was at Palace Station on a recent evening when, as usual, it was virtually impossible to find a quarter or dollar machine available. Yet, over a three-hour period, I could have had my selection of fifty cent machines at any time because hardly a soul was playing them.

Nonetheless, the possibilities offered by the fifty cent slots are intriguing and I will soon check them out somewhere. Meantime, I continue to watch them with more than a little interest.

Quarters are universally the most popular denomination.

Most casinos have two, three, even four times as many quarter slots as dollar machines. The payback percentages compare reasonably well, generally in the range of 0.5 percent to 0.75 percent less at around 95.2 percent average in competitive locations. This means that the player has a fair chance of keeping losses in check and because of the huge amount of daily play these machines get, even making money.

I prefer to work dollar slots myself but my experience is that the strategies in this book can be applied to either quarter or dollar machines.

Remember the Rule of 80 which says 80 percent of slot players will lose 80 percent of their money 80 percent of the time? If the best you do in a casino betters the Rule of 80, you will be a winner of sorts.

On either quarter or dollar slots and probably fifty cent machines, find the right mix of numbers and players, adopt the appropriate work approach, and you should have a realistic chance of cashing in.

TYPES OF MACHINES

Pay Lines

The most common slots are single pay line machines with the pay line horizontal across the center of the symbol windows. Get a row of winning symbols on this line when the reels stop spinning and you have some money coming back.

Single pay line machines will prominently display the message All Pays on Center Line Only.

Among every group of slots, you will find several which seem identical in appearance until you take a closer look and see that, instead of a single line, these machines may have three pay lines or more.

The three liners are popular among many slot players because they appear to offer three times as many winning chances. Not so!

Symbol combinations on any line can win and the reels can stop with winners on two or even all three lines, generally bars and blanks. Since the slots pay out on all winning lines, you can often get a double or triple dip from a single spin.

That can be fun, but don't be tricked into thinking you will do better on three liners than on single pay line machines. Examine that pay board closely. You will find, similar to the option-buy slots I describe in more detail later in this chapter, you must play extra coins to activate those additional pay lines. Where the second and third coins buy extra winning combinations on an option-buy slot, here they buy more pay lines.

To further complicate matters, there are also three line option buy slots where, for instance, the first two coins activate bars but not sevens. You must play three coins to have all three lines and all winning symbols going for you.

Many nickel machines and some quarter machines have five pay lines, three horizontals, and two diagonals. As with the three liners, you must play five coins to reap any reward from winners on the fifth line.

There is another pay line variation you should know about. I don't know the official term for this variation but we could call it the Any Position Compensation Pay. Machines with this feature have appeared in more casinos over the past two or three years.

These slots pay out when certain symbols appear anywhere on the glass. For example, two wild cards above or below the center pay line and one on the line may return one hundred coins. Had all three been on the pay line, the return may have been four hundred, one thousand, or maybe ten thousand, coins depending on the machine and the number of coins played. This feature can be found on both single and multiple pay line machines.

Before leaving this section, I want to comment on the near-miss phenomenon.

Except on machines that feature Any Position Compensation Pay, the player gets nothing when the slot lines up winning symbols above or below the pay line. This happens a lot. I have lost count of the times I've seen jackpot symbols lined up in a tantalizing row everywhere but in the right place.

These are not near misses, nor are they harbingers of rich rewards to come. Because of the relationship between the RNG, the game program, and the reel strips, it is inevitable that the most coveted symbols occasionally show up in different positions on the glass. Less valuable or losing combinations do so much more frequently. The difference is you always notice when it happens with the symbols which bring money; you don't notice the others.

Several years ago a line of slots designed to tease players with deliberate near misses were introduced into the market by the manufacturer of the popular Magnificent Sevens, the Universal Company. Those machines have been outlawed. Once again, there is no such thing as a true near miss on slot machines no matter what you think you see.

Now let's move on to examine more of the differences among the slots we find in modern casinos.

Number of Reels

Three reel machines dominate the casino landscape but, if you are tempted by big contraptions or even bigger dreams, you may find yourself staring at four, five, six, or even seven reels.

The measurement of odds used in bygone days could provide a fairly meaningful comparison of the respective merits of three, four, and five reelers. On slots with twenty stops per reel, so-called experts calculated jackpot odds as twenty to the power of the number of reels out to an astronomical one in 3,200,000 if the machine had five reels.

This was an imprecise measure even in the days of mechanical slots because few people really knew how many times the jackpot symbols appeared on any reel. But it was a breeze compared to trying a similar calculation today. In the age of microchips, RNGs, and theoretical stops as high as 256 per reel, the odds of hitting any single stop combination could stretch the digital readout of most calculators beyond capacity.

You can assume your win prospects probably diminish in proportion to the increase in the number of reels, although one executive has told me players in his casino have as much chance of winning on four reel machines as they do on three reelers.

My questions to manufacturers on this point have gone unanswered. Nonetheless, since I don't see many three reelers on the wide area progressives or at other locations offering million dollar jackpots, I think I am justified in concluding an ordinary guy like me should stick to three reel machines for general daily activity.

Multipliers

Multipliers are the most common but not always the most popular slots in the casino. Two factors attract me: Except for the jackpot and, rarely, the second top line, there is no penalty for playing less than maximum coins—each coin will buy a multiple of each winning payout; and irrespective of how many coins I elect to play, all winning symbols on the header board will pay out. There are no unpleasant surprises.

I know some people have the idea they should always play maximum coins on multipliers rather than take the risk of hitting the jackpot with only one coin in.

I am happy to scttlc for $400, $1,000, or $2,000 back from one coin, since it is unlikely I will hit a jackpot without any previous win—which could have brought me to the two coin investment level in an aggressive work plan.

This happened to me late on a recent visit. Red, white, and blue sevens came up and I collected $400 instead of the $1,000 I would have received with two coins in. The win could not have come at a more opportune time. I had been through a series of break-even or losing sessions and was well down at that stage.

When I looked at my daily activity record, I counted my blessings as well as the money. The figures showed that, had I been playing maximum coins instead of the step-up strategy I was using, I would have been wiped out long before I reached the tenth session in my twelve session day.

Instead, I completed the allotted sessions, picked up a small win and a smaller loss on the last two sessions, and cancelled out my losses for the day, finishing $360 ahead.

Great fun! The Windows of Opportunity had worked for me only because I was not playing maximum coins each spin on the multiplier machines I was working that day.

Option-buy Machines

Option-buys have been called many names, most unprintable—especially when what appears to be a winning combination doesn't return a cent. I have heard technicians refer to these machines as buy pays, player's choice, or symbol adders.

Player's choice is a misnomer because too often players do not realize they must choose whether to play the whole payboard or just part of it.

I call these slots *aggregators* because each coin brings only a part of the header board into play. The aggregation can be activated only with maximum coins. However, in this book I refer to them as option buys because this seems to be the name commonly used in the industry.

Instead of buying bigger payouts with each additional coin, option buy slots give you more winning symbols. You must play maximum coins to cover the entire pay board or risk seeing the bigger combinations hit and return nothing.

We described Magnificent Sevens in the last chapter as an example of an option buy machine with a simple, readable header board. A fair argument can be made that this was not the best example to use because this slot is not an option buy in the strictest sense.

Magnificent Sevens is a hybrid—part multiplier, part option buy. The second coin doubles the payout on bars or blanks as with a regular multiplier and only the third coin will bring sevens into play.

If you are prepared to ignore sevens and accept only four payback combinations above money-back, you can play one or two coins just like a regular two coin multiplier without fear of being penalized for your thrift.

True option buy machines offer additional payout symbols on the second, third, fourth, and fifth coins, if the slot accepts that many. As a group, especially if there is a high number of possible payout combinations, option buys have busy pay boards which can be deceptive because the symbols bought with the extra coins often look remarkably similar to those which pay out on the first coin.

Take time to sit down and study those header boards to be sure you know precisely what you are buying with each coin. To tap the bigger payouts, you must play maximum coins every spin. This is the only way to give yourself a fair chance of conserving your stake and winning.

That's not enough for me. My daily stake and loss limits per visit are not enough to buy the Windows of Opportunity and the ratio of worthwhile payouts I would need to play option buys. I watch others play and I wish them luck but that is the extent of my interest.

Progressive Jackpot Slot Machines

When the biggest payout increases with the volume of play, we call it a progressive slot.

In progressives the accent is on the jackpot. Over a given number of pay cycles, the total payback, including the jackpot, will meet the manufacturer's specified percentages and thus comply with gaming regulations. On that basis alone, you can guess that the return from regular play is going to be less than on most other types of slots. Unless you are a top line hunter and don't care how much money you lose, this would be reason enough to avoid progressive machines. However, the actual spin-to-spin win potential is cut further by a set-aside called the escrow account.

No progressive jackpot starts at zero dollars. Who would play if it did? The start size must attract players and that lead-in money has to come from somewhere. As casinos have no control over when jackpots will be hit, a percentage of each dollar played will be taken out and put into escrow to fund those progressive jackpots. This way the casinos avoid a financial crisis in the event a huge jackpot is struck first day out or before enough money has accumulated to cover the payout from actual play.

The casino still takes its win out of the pool. The escrow lets the casino set aside a bigger slice than may be required since the increasing jackpot is likely to represent a bigger portion of the total payback percentage. So what does all this mean? It means the prospects of making money from routine payouts will be a lot less on progressive machines than on other slots.

Add the fact that you must play maximum coins each spin to have any prospect of winning the jackpot and you can see there are plenty of reasons to pass on progressives.

Until recent years, most progressive jackpots were on stand-alone machines or grouped. Then came the inter-casino variations where slots in several locations, often under the same ownership, were linked together to permit accumulation of much bigger jackpots.

Once among the most popular machines in casinos, stand-alone progressives have now lost most of their appeal. Their jackpots fall mainly into two categories: small amounts which are won frequently and are often less than the fixed top line payouts on multiplier and option buy slots; or much bigger prizes which suggest, since there is only one machine feeding the pool, a win is imminent or the odds of hitting are way out in Never-Never Land.

The size of a big jackpot on a stand-alone progressive has long been considered by some canny gamblers to be a reliable indicator of the chances of actually winning it.

The theory goes something like this: If 1 percent of the money going through the machine was being allocated to the jackpot pool, then the bigger the jackpot the greater the number of losing spins already tallied. By default, the slot would be that much closer to payout time. For example, if the jackpot showed $10,000, it would have taken 333,000 spins, or $1 million, to reach that point (at 1¢ per $1 played assuming the maximum three coins per spin).

On an old twenty-four stop, four reel machine, the odds of hitting the jackpot combination would be one in 331,776—less than the number of spins logged since the slot last hit the big prize. Simple arithmetic, according to that logic, suggests the slot must be close to paying out again and is worth playing.

The problem with this theory is that nothing has ever been quite so simple in the slot world, not even in the good old days. Assuming the one in 331,776 odds were correct, those odds would apply as much to each future spin as they had to all spins past. There was absolutely no way to predict how much more money would be required to buy the next jackpot.

Slot machine odds are not like the odds in certain card games where cards are discarded as they are drawn until so few remain that the winning hand is assured. Were that the case, we could all make money until the casinos went out of business!

Numerologists can safely state that if a given result has not come up over a certain number of spins, chances are greater it will come up within the next sequence. What mathematicians cannot tell you is whether it will happen sooner or later in any given sequence nor how long the run must be extended before the combination will hit.

* * * *

A lot of money has been won on stand-alone progressive slots in the past using the jackpot measurement theory. To all practical purposes, the rationale is alive and well today and applies to a greater or lesser extent to all types of progressive machines.

Yet, as logical as it may sound, the theory guarantees nothing. Prudent players will stay away from any progressive slot until the amount is significantly higher than the top-line payouts offered on regular stand-alone machines where there is no rolling meter to indicate how much play has gone through since the last big payout. Let other people spend money to build those whopper jackpots.

In my opinion, if you are looking for the big kill, a much better gauge on any progressive slot is the historical size of the jackpot.

Make inquiries. Find out how much was paid out when the machine last hit and the time before and the time before that.

The amounts will be different but my guess is that most jackpots which have paid out several times at around $5,000 in the past will probably hit near that mark regularly.

My advice is this—don't even think about entering the fray until the jackpot on that beckoning progressive machine is at least as high as the lowest previous payout level. I would go further. The jackpot would have to be higher than any previous payout to tempt me.

Double pool, stand alone, progressive jackpot machines can still be found in most casinos, generally at the end of a carousel or literally standing by themselves somewhere else.

These versions, which should not be confused with WAPS machines which offer secondary pools, have not one but two separate jackpot meters. Play alternates between them. When you insert your coins, an arrow will indicate which jackpot pool has been activated.

A question I have heard asked occasionally is "do you win both pools if you play two coins?" The answer is no. Two coins buys neither. You must play maximum coins on any progressive to have any chance of winning either jackpot and, although it makes no difference to the result, it is a good idea to look up and see which pool is in play before you push the Play Maximum Coins button.

Multi-machine and carousel progressives are the intermediate stage between stand alones and inter-casino progressive jackpot slots. These can have as few as two or three machines feeding a common pool or literally dozens in the same group— or in combination with other machines located elsewhere in the casino.

Unlike stand-alone progressives which usually have the jackpot meter sited on the slot, multi-feed systems are easily located by prominent displays telegraphing the size of the progressive pool. State gaming regulations require these signs above each group.

Apart from the larger jackpots which are typical of such installations, the principal differences between group and stand alones lie in the volume of play they get and the competition among the machines for the same jackpot.

Which brings us to another caveat. I have been privy to several discussions where people have mistakenly thought that, with a concerted group effort, they could cover all machines and significantly improve their prospects of hitting the jackpot.

I suppose that makes sense in a kind of quasi-logical way, especially if the display is showing a reward much higher than the historical pay point. However, assuming the jackpot is already high enough to justify a group attack, there are probably other slots in the casino feeding this same pool.

Covering a stand of four machines when there are twenty

others in the same system does not give you much protection and could cost you and your friends big bucks.

The danger of making an error in judgment is greater when the jackpot is inter-casino. There is no way to tell how many machines are pushing those jackpot numbers.

Watch the climbing totals. If the figures are rolling upwards at a speed faster than people are inserting coins in the slots you can see, there must be other machines in the pool; if those increases are much faster, other casinos are probably linked into the system.

WIDE AREA PROGRESSIVE SLOTS

Computerization has brought the capacity to expand the inter-casino progressive concept to hundreds of casinos. Participating casinos can be on the same street, in the same city, statewide, or theoretically thousands of miles apart.

The introduction of Wide Area Progressive Slots (or WAPS) has revolutionized the industry and created a whole new attack of headaches for regulators.

An inspiration of Sy Redd, the founder of International Game Technology (IGT) which owns and operates the most ubiquitous systems, WAPS, with their huge jackpots running into the millions, are already dominating the casino scene.

The best known are Nevada Nickels, Quartermania, and Megabucks but recent additions include Fabulous 50s (maybe an acknowledgment from industry insiders that their research indicates increasing popularity for 50 cent machines), and High Rollers which, true to its name, starts with a $500,000 base on $5 slots and, in addition to the money, rewards its winners with the keys to a luxury automobile.

As of June, 1994, the Megabucks statewide system in Nevada comprised 748 machines in 134 casinos and had produced 31 winners who, on paper at least, became millionaires; Nevada Nickels, with a base jackpot of $200,000, linked 1,380 machines; and Quartermania, a two level jackpot game starting at $400,000, was available on more than 1,100 machines throughout the state.

Although the chances of winning are the same on any machine in the WAPS systems, it is noteworthy that, at the time I checked, the three biggest payouts were won at Harrah's Casinos, in Las Vegas, Reno, and Lake Tahoe. A remarkable coincidence, given the number of casinos offering WAPS, but I wager that those huge wins have attracted a lot of new slots business for the Promus Companies.

Despite the success at Harrah's, there are more zeros in the odds against striking a WAPS jackpot than there are in the telephone directory; a little exaggeration, I know, but to describe them as remote would be an indulgent assessment.

Every man, woman, and child has one chance in 16,000 of being struck by lightning in his or her lifetime and several million chances against being hit on any given day. Well, compared to the odds of winning a WAPS bonanza, we are all more likely to be struck by lightning half a dozen times before breakfast tomorrow. You have a much better chance of winning your state lottery with a single ticket.

The lure of riches from these huge jackpots has spread far beyond Nevada, the home base of IGT. Separate Megabucks systems are now operating in Atlantic City, Mississippi, Louisiana, and several other states, with more in the advanced planning stages, and also in overseas locations.

While WAPS systems are wonderful money-earners for the stockholders of IGT, a public company, they are a mixed blessing for others, not only for gaming authorities but also for the casinos and the players.

In moments of candor, several slots managers have acknowledged that the popularity of WAPS systems has thrust them into a Catch 22 position. Customer pressure dictates that they must offer the jackpots in their casinos or they will lose business to competitors; thus they are being forced into diverting considerable cash flow from machines, where each casino retains its full percentage, to WAPS where the casino hold must be shared with the system operators.

Since there is a minimum win casinos must collect from each group of devices and games to survive, this means that the total percentage deducted for the combined casino-IGT win in any location will be higher than for other slots of the same denomination.

Of course, the few fortunate players who have beaten the galactic odds and won millions of dollars on WAPS jackpots are counting their blessings. Yet, even among this group, we do not need a sensitive nose to detect a faint taint of disenchantment.

Why? As with winners in most state lotteries, WAPS winners do not receive all those millions up front. They are paid out in annual instalments over 20 years. Although the regulations require a notice on all machines which do not pay the full jackpot in cash immediately, the significance is lost on many winners until after the event when they receive their first check and find it is for ¹⁄₂₀th (less withholding tax) of their incredible windfall.

Instead of getting the full amount to deposit in the bank, a six million dollar winner will receive a check for about $216,000 after tax, less than the purchase price of a luxury home. It can be a moment of sobering reality for anybody.

Where WAPS differ from state lotteries is in the way that payout is calculated. It is here that WAPS have created the biggest controversy. When a state lottery announces the next jackpot, the figure is based on the total annuity payments which all the money in the winner pool will buy. The lottery is not already holding the full jackpot amount in escrow.

The progressive slots jackpot, however, does not use the entire amount of money already accumulated from every dollar which has gone into every machine in the system since the last jackpot was paid. Unlike the lottery, if the display on a WAPS stand is showing six million dollars, that is the amount which has already been collected and is in escrow.

Critics of extended payouts—and I make no apologies for being vociferous among them—contend that there is no valid reason why the entire pool should not be paid out immediately.

Should some regulatory agency decide, in its wisdom, that instant payout of such huge sums is undesirable, then the annual payments should at least distribute the FULL proceeds of the annuity which can be purchased with ALL the money in the pool.

What difference would this make to a winner? It more than doubles the take. From an 8 percent annuity, it would increase the amount our six million dollar man would be getting before tax each year from $300,000 to over $611,000, or a gross payout of close to $12,225,000 instead of the $6,000,000 he has to wait twenty years to receive under the present authorized WAPS payout procedures.

An 8 percent annuity returning $300,000 for 20 years can be bought for as little as $2,945,000. So, unwittingly, our jackpot winner is giving away more than half the present day capital value of his huge win before he or she even gets to think about distributing any of the largess among family or friends. Do you think he would voluntarily do this?

So who is pocketing the cash left in the jackpot pool after the annuity has been bought? In the WAPS systems, the big winner is the owner of the games, International Game Technology, which in addition to its percentage cut as the operator, is winning big each time the jackpot is hit.

IGT is not at fault here. Who can blame the company for devising a system which would boost its profits for the foreseeable future? This was a brilliant piece of forward revenue planning on the part of Sy Redd which, from a purely business point of view, should be applauded.

Unfortunately, the strategy works much better for the major stockholders in IGT than it does for the individuals who share in WAPS jackpots.

It has also created a market opportunity for a competitor.

Casino Data Systems, a Las Vegas-based relative newcomer to the manufacturing scene. Until recently, CDS was best known in the industry as the systems company which developed OASIS, the sophisticated tracking program used by many casinos to monitor machine performance and customer activity. Now the company has entered the WAPS market with Cool Millions, which offers $1,000,000 in immediate cash to jackpot winners with the balance paid out over 20 years.

A final point to remember. I am told that Megabucks and other WAPS jackpots have been struck several times with less than maximum coins played. What a devastating mistake! On one of those occasions, the pool was over $8,000,000.

For some reason, the player, a woman in this case, had apparently been playing two coins instead of three for several hours before the Megabucks symbols lined up across the payline. The consolation prize, for hitting the jackpot with two coins in, did not console her or her irate husband. His reaction was violent. She had forfeited eight million dollars with her two coin play.

Heed the lesson! If you play progressive slots, come to the machines with sufficient money in hand to play all-coins-in *every spin*. When there, stay alert, watch what is happening, and *always* use the Play Maximum Coins button.

HOUSE MACHINES

Most casinos have at least one bay of custom-built slots.

Since the philosophy of casino management, almost without exception, is to encourage patrons to play maximum coins at all times, these house machines are mostly the option-buy type which I generally avoid.

Sometimes, they are stand-alone slots but in many places you will find them linked into carousels or bays which feed progressive jackpots.

At the risk of sounding ambivalent, I must say that I view option-buy house machines in a more favorable light.

Why? The house machine is serving a dual function. Not only is it a profits center, as are all other slots in the establishment, but it is also a promotional tool which prominently displays the casino name, logo, the dominant theme of the establishment, or perhaps the name of the major show attraction. It is because of this second function that I take a closer look at these slots, especially in casinos where they are grouped together in full rows or carousels.

Casinos would much rather have you win $500 than hit the top line and get $5,000 or $10,000. This is not because they don't like winners. They do! A golden rule in the casino industry is that the more winners there are in a group of players, the more money the whole group will spend, and the more money the casino will take out. Contrary to popular perception, casinos like paying out winners but the ones they really love to pay are those mid-size amounts. They would prefer to see the $10,000 in that top line jackpot paid out in smaller amounts among ten or twenty people rather than to one lucky individual.

Their motives for preferring a lot of smaller winners to a single big winner are strictly business-related. The casino knows that it has an excellent chance of getting all of those $500 or $1,000 wins back, and more, from players whose appetite is whetted and who stay on to stretch their luck. It has little hope of getting much of that $10,000 when it goes to one winner.

The statistics confirm that most large jackpot winners go home with the bulk of the money they have won. As the figures also show that a high percentage of them will not return more than once or twice during the next five years, when that big winner walks out the door, the money goes too.

Yet casinos need big winners to create enthusiasm, passion, and illusion, to attract more customers and to induce their regulars to keep coming back.

What better way to achieve this than to compromise on the

size of the top line payouts and link as many as possible directly to the casino name, logo, or theme?

They can do this when they place their orders for house machines, by opting for jackpots around the $1,000 mark and specifying the loosest game programs available.

It is not unusual for these custom-built slots to have the highest percentage paybacks in the casino and offer the best pay frequencies, with payboards weighted towards producing a higher number of those top line wins.

When you hit that 1,000 coin jackpot on Jackpots Galore at the Riviera, or the progressive jackpot on the Ho-Waiian Luau carousel at the Westward Ho, or the stand alone or the progressive Lion's Share or Majestic Lions slots at, you guessed it, the MGM Grand, you win—and so does the casino.

Let us tick off some of the ways the casino benefits:

- enough jackpots will be won on these machines every day to induce patrons to play maximum coins; the average revenue per spin jumps from around 2.1 coins to three at these locations;
- the frequency of jackpots will attract more players and entice them to these locations; in turn, this ensures the machines will continue to generate jackpot wins at an accelerated rate and continuous maximum coins play for longer periods
- the median size jackpots mean there is a much better chance that many of these winners will stay on and play elsewhere in the casino;
- those who "take the money and run" have won on machines identified with only one casino; when they come back, they will return to their lucky spot and the same slots; more importantly, when they tell others about their big wins, they will be talking about winning on machines which are not found elsewhere—a super endorsement!

There have been as many as sixteen progressive jackpot hits in a single day on the Ho-Waiian Luau carousel at the Westward Ho. I have sat at the deli and watched three come up within one hour on a busy day.

The start figure for the jackpot is $1,000. The lowest payout I have seen is $1,003. Most times, it pays out at plus or minus $1,100. Once I saw it reach $1,360 before being hit.

Since there are only twenty machines on the carousel, the player who takes the time to work the figures will agree that, provided he or she is prepared to play $3 per spin, five or six spins per minute, and stay there for at least an hour when all machines are in use, the odds of winning one of those jackpots are probably no worse than 20 to 1.

Given an expenditure of $15 per minute for a total of $900 per hour, and a probable return of say 60 percent by way of smaller hits, then the theoretical cost of playing this progressive slot is likely to be around $360 per hour of play.

This is about double the down side in my more aggressive Work Plans for two coin multipliers but where else can you reduce the odds of winning $1,000 on one spin to about 20 to 1? It is an attractive tradeoff.

The Jackpots Galore house machines at the Riviera are not linked to a progressive jackpot. Yet the payout situation there and at the MGM Grand is much the same. These stand alone machines produce many jackpot winners every day. There are many instances on file of the same house machines paying multiple jackpots within a twenty-four hour period.

In the last chapter, when we discussed the key features to look for in your target machines, we stressed the relative importance of payback percentages, strength in the payboard, and pay frequencies. We also recommended that you concentrate your efforts on multipliers.

Well, most house machines are not multipliers but what you are giving up on the one hand, you may be making up for on the other. Payback percentages are likely to be among the best in the casino. The header boards, though decidedly weighted towards the top line payout, are strong enough, and the pay frequencies high enough (as much as one to six overall) to offset the inherent disadvantages of option-buy machines.

If you are prepared to risk more money and play maximum coins per spin continuously on house machines, chances are you may lose more than you would following one of my Work Plans but I would be hard put to find you better odds of winning $1,000 from a single strike.

11

The Keys to Winland— and the Padlocks That Keep You Out

Play maximum coins! That is the advice you are likely to get when you seek guidance from so-called experts. You don't have to look far, the exhortation is on every slot machine.

Well, I challenge that counsel. You may be committed to a compulsive hunt for some massive progressive jackpot and don't care how much you lose. But playing maximum coins spin after spin, session after session, day after day, is a sure way to wipe out your stake.

There will be occasional special situations when you will make a decision to play all coins in. As a strategy for keeping your losses under control and improving your chances of making a little money during everyday play, however, the practice is akin to buying groceries with cash from the local loan shark—not too smart.

The writers and experts justify their recommendations with the lame rationale that those who play maximum coins are rewarded with higher percentage paybacks. Technically, that is correct, but we have already established that those higher paybacks are most often the result of a premium in the top line payout, or of having more symbols in play.

Since my strategies concentrate on mid-level wins on multipliers, the odds of hitting any payback combination are no better with three coins in than they are with one—except playing with three coins in would swallow my money faster.

I understand why casinos preach the maximum coins philosophy. I would, too, if I owned the slot machines. The more dollars you can be cajoled into playing per spin, the more profit there will be on the bottom line of the casino operating statement at the end of the month.

Irrespective of whether I win or lose, my strategies cost the casinos.

In a typical twelve session day, using the Green Plan, I will invest $600. The average number of spins per session will be between forty-five and forty-six, a total of around 540 to 550 spins for the day, and a mean of 1.1 coins played per spin.

In about two hours time, assuming my activity is confined to 95 percent payback slots, the house win is only $15 per hour when I use the Green Plan. At that rate, I would have to stay more than six hours for the casino to reach its $100 daily target from in-residence customers.

Compare that with a patron playing maximum coins on a three coin machine for the same number of spins over the same two-hour period. That player will put $1,620 through the machine (to my $600) and the casino take will soar to $81. Most players average five to six spins per minute against my 4.5. At this faster pace, maximum coins each spin will increase cash in play to $2,160 and the casino win climbs to $108. These players have not improved their winning chances but the casino has done very well.

Few players are brash enough to bring a $2,000 stake to the slots each day. Assume then that the three coin player arrives with the same $600 stake I do. *That player must recover the stake, plus a 260 percent profit* just to have enough cash in hand to keep the Windows of Opportunity open for the same number of spins I am buying with my $600.

That is a Texas-size tall order! When I start out, I know my stake will get me through all twelve sessions. *I am not depending on making three times my money just to hang in long enough to give me the number of winning chances experience tells me I need.*

When I make 260 percent, or even 160 percent on my money, be assured most of it will finish up in my pocket at the end of the day and not in the belly of a ravenous slot machine.

The choice is yours. It is more than a philosophy; it may be a question of survival. Let's sum up:

In the Green Plan, with a daily purse of $600, the casino hold is fixed at $30, your downside risk is strictly limited, and you have a **guarantee** you will complete twelve machine sessions over one and a half to two hours.

You will get as many as six hundred opportunities to hit that one combination per session or day which safeguards your stake and gives you a fair chance to make money. Unless you are already in profit, you have fifty spin chances at each machine.

Alternatively, you could play maximum coins, bestow a much bigger win on the casino (up to $108), risk all your stake, and have no guarantee you will be around long enough to complete even half your sessions unless you have won your stake back plus 50 percent. To keep the Windows of Opportunity open for full sessions on all twelve machines, you must play $1,560 more than you brought with you, i.e., you need that profit of 260 percent just to see you through the day.

♠ **The only time to play maximum coins in regular play is when payout prospects are at their peak! All other times you are wasting your money.**

The adage, a time and a place for everything, applies to slot strategies, too.

A feature common to each of the work plans in this book is the control and timing of when to play additional coins.

By restricting our efforts to two coin machines, we eliminate the third coin risk immediately and a second step-up stage.

By establishing start and end points for when we go to two coins and when we drop back to single coin play, we set definite limits on the amount of money we can lose at any machine session and the length of time we will stay there.

Time is the casino's ally. It is no accident there are no clocks in a casino. The longer you stay at the slots, the more you will lose and the more the casino is going to make, directly or indirectly.

On my last trip to Las Vegas, I watched a man who was enjoying an incredible run of luck on a two coin dollar machine. He had started with a $100 slide. His style of play was methodical and he began with a single coin and played ten or twelve spins until he struck double bars, at which point he went to two coin play.

As so often happens, the next payout followed quickly. Within two spins, he hit again, another set of double bars, then treble bars, and mixed sevens courtesy of the wild card symbol. He was on a great run and was keeping his credits in the machine. So far so good. He looked over at me and commented that this was going to be one big wonderful day. He was an out-of-towner and had never had a winning day in four previous visits to this casino.

I watched that man more than three hours and recorded my observations. The episode is worth comment for there are several lessons to be learned.

I doubt whether I have seen such an extended sequence of generous payouts. One after another they came. As he was playing off the credit meter and had not touched the slugs in his slide again, it was easy to keep tabs on his progress despite a pronounced acceleration in his speed of play.

When I left him to go to an appointment, the streak was at an end and he was back using the coins in the slide. There were a few credits left on the meter but he had decided to leave them there and play what was left of his stake.

At the peak of his winning streak, he had accumulated more than $600 on the meter but he did not cash in. The credit meter was down, then up again. My notes indicate it edged below $200 then soared back over the $500 mark at least five times.

The player knew this was his big day and the top line was commanding him to stay. By the time I left, my calculations showed he had run close to $3,500 through a two coin slot, an incredible feat of consistent winning. The casino's take was around $175, and he was about to exhaust the money he had left.

When I returned, I asked the carousel attendant what had happened. The man lasted only a few minutes after I departed and, sure enough, he had lost the rest of his $100.

Note this. Had he risked only his $100 stake and taken his money out then, he would have had that wonderful winning day he was seeking and the casino hold would have been around $5. Several times, he could have departed with at least $500 to $600 in profits.

He stayed. Instead of being a winner, he gave the casino $175—his start money plus 75 percent—and only because he played and replayed every payback dollar he won.

Now $500 or $600 is a lot of money, especially if you come in with only $100. Few of us get many chances to pocket that sort of change in a few hours. So what went wrong?

Juiced by his run of luck, he elected to stay and shoot for the big hit. At the end of one of the longest streaks of midsize wins I have seen, he had given the casino what it covets most from every player who comes through the door—time! The gift of time is the gift of money. He may as well have written a check.

The player made four costly mistakes which, unfortunately, are made every day, in every casino:

1. He targeted the top line jackpot as his goal.
2 He stayed at the machine far beyond the huge Windows

of Opportunity he had been given.
3. He played off the credits instead of his stake.
4. He had absolutely no strategy or plan for leaving the slot with his winnings intact.

I think he made another error. As though mesmerized by the frequency of hits when he did well, he played the machine at breakneck speed. He did not take care.

The four work plans address each of these dangerous situations. They are not guaranteed to produce winning days every time you go the casino but, even if you decide against using the strategies and devise your own, your winning prospects will be dramatically improved when you adopt and stay with the underlying principles expounded in this book.

I have three more recommendations before we discuss record keeping, keys, and padlocks.

Wear comfortable clothes with plenty of pockets. You should have a convenient place for your pen and your daily activity record. You also need a pocket for your identification card and, if you join the casino slot club, for that card too.

As you will be taking out the daily activity record and club card at every session, you should make a point of keeping your money in other pockets.

Since I am convinced you now have the capacity to win more and win often, I suggest you use two pockets for your notes, one for your daily stake, the other for your winnings.

Never mix the two. Stake is stake. Winnings are winnings.

The next hints relate to physical management of your money while you are in the casino.

There is no need to convert your entire bankroll into dollar slugs or quarters. I start off with one $100 slide for dollar slots; three $10 rolls (120 coins) for quarter machines. When you need more, you can get more.

Before you start play at any machine, be certain you have enough coins or slugs in hand to complete the session without interruption.

Avoid the temptation to wing it when you have strung a few losing runs together and are reluctant to buy more slugs in the belief the next slot will prove positive. You may be right but my best guess is there is a greater chance you will become tentative and will conserve your coins when you get down to those last lonely survivors in the bucket.

In addition to the slide or bucket of coins you buy from the cashier, you should arm yourself with several empty receptacles—one for the money you have allocated to the machine you are playing and at least one other for the winnings you are holding.

Make it a practice to cash in regularly and put the notes in the pocket you have reserved for your winnings. It makes no sense to haul a lot of slugs around. If you win several hundred dollars in a session, cash in immediately.

Full dollar slides can get very heavy. They also attract attention. I would rather cash lots of $200, and bring a single slide to the next session rather than wait until I am struggling with four or five slides.

When you need to replenish your slug supply, be sure to take the money from your daily bankroll. Do not take it from the pocket which has your cash winnings.

Play from your stake at all times, not from the winnings bucket. Do not play the credits in the machine except when the strategy calls for an overrun into part of your interim winnings during a session.

Cash those credits only at the end of a session. Should the slot automatically fire out a big win, put the slugs into slides, complete the session, then cash out. Even when you hit a hand-paid win, complete the session before you take the credits out of the machine.

To stay in full control, you must be alert at all times.

My first visit to a casino was in Sydney, Australia, many years ago. A friend invited me to the St. George's Rugby League Club one evening and, though I had no interest in slot machines at that time, I had heard so much about this wicked place I thought it would be a great idea to see what was happening.

What I saw was a turnoff. I did not return to another casino for more than twenty years.

The slots players seemed mesmerized—automatons, lost in a rhythmic trance, picking coins from the trays, feeding them into the slots, pulling the levers, picking more coins out, feeding them in again, on and on without taking their eyes from the reel glass. Even when the machines paid out, the cycle went on without interruption.

I must say that, though I have since seen people so engrossed they might not notice the ceiling collapsing, I have not encountered any casino scene like that at the St. George's Club in Sydney.

My practice is to stop and start. Even in the middle of a machine session, I stand up, stretch, look around at what other people are doing, have a cup of coffee or fruit juice, and gather my thoughts.

Moving from machine to machine at regular intervals also helps keep me alert and often I will deliberately take time out between sessions to wander around for a few minutes. Occasionally I cash in and go outside for some fresh air.

These breaks are brief but revitalizing. Whether I happen to be winning or losing, I am better prepared mentally when I sit at the next machine.

The work plans in the next chapter have triggers and release points for moving from single coin play to maximum coins and returning. They also have set protocols for determining when to exit each machine.

I should warn you that none of these parameters is fail-safe. They are predicated to some extent on which of the three goals discussed earlier is perceived by each reader to be his or her primary motivation in trying slots.

Before choosing which plan to follow or creating your own adaptation, you must decide what is more important: protecting your capital with a conservative strategy, or exposing yourself to the risk of greater losses in return for an increased chance of making money. It is a trade-off. I am convinced you cannot have it both ways.

The Silver, Gold, and Emerald plans are progressively more aggressive than the Green Plan. They also demand more vigilance. The prospect of winning is greatest with the Emerald Plan, but it is more complicated to follow and the downside risk is higher.

Novice players should start with one of the less difficult plans until they have developed an understanding of the various protocols, the signals, and the responses.

Without question there will be times when you revert from two coin play to one coin and the next spin comes up with a good win. Do not fret. It happens the other way, too, and I am confident you will gain more with the money you save than you will lose by not picking up the additional value of those occasional untimely hits. The compensations more than make up for the exasperation.

My experience is that, despite the deliberately random scatter of the technology, there is a payout pattern of sorts on all machines. The RNG has a reference feature which allows it to check back on the two previous spins but it has no memory of what has gone before. Play and payout functions are handled by other chips in the configuration. So not even the machine itself can predict precisely when a slot will hit or what it will hit.

Nonetheless, many times the payouts seem to come in batches, and it is not unusual for long breaks between hits. I have struck back-to-back sevens several times and repeat sevens and bars within five spins too often to be explained any other way. I have also gone forty spins and more without a single hit.

The objectives in all our work plans are: to benefit from the spin sequences which bring you money; to avoid those which cost you money; and to leave each session without extending your losses or threatening your winnings.

We will not be able to achieve those objectives every time we visit a casino. When we play slot machines, we are literally playing the numbers. Sometimes the numbers will be right, sometimes wrong, but the confidence which comes from using any system lies in realizing that, if the rationale is correct and the reasoning logical, the odds of striking more often will always be in our favor.

Keeping adequate records of any gambling activity involves more than merely jotting down a few numbers when you happen to win. To be of any value, records should be kept daily and should reflect all slot activity.

When I started this slot machine exercise, I brought a positive mental attitude to my tasks. This was a vital and intrinsic part of my planning and preparation.

Since I was convinced I was going to win, I knew I must keep timely, accurate records from the outset—records which would satisfy the Internal Revenue Service and allow me to review my activities, by the session, by the day, and by the visit. Only that way would I have the information to enable me to make adjustments in my approach when appropriate and to keep a watch on what was working for me and what was not.

Failure to keep records is the most basic mistake among people who find they are suddenly obliged to report gambling winnings on their tax returns. This generally happens as the result of a big win when they are faced with the reality that, no matter what they may have lost before the win, the casino is obliged to report the winning event to the IRS.

No use crying foul because you have no tangible record of

what you have lost previously. Just as the burden is on the casino to detail your big wins, the onus is on you to prove any losses you are entitled to claim against the reported wins.

Since even the most clairvoyant among us cannot predict if, when, or what we are likely to win in any given year, there is only one way to handle this situation. Be prepared!

♠ **From the first time you walk into any casino, keep adequate and accurate records of every wagering transaction.**

Tax law permits you to deduct gambling losses incurred in years you report winnings, up to the full amount of those winnings.

The IRS does not exhibit any particular goodwill or benevolence toward gamblers. It is suspicious of returns which claim large losses to offset winnings reports the casino filed on your behalf. The IRS is likely to ask you to substantiate those losses, to prove they are not figments of imagination conjured the day you realized you would have to pay tax on your winnings.

Experience tells them big wins are not the exclusive domain of inveterate gamblers; as often as not they are likely to be struck by casual players.

Unless you have supporting documents which will hold up under scrutiny, the IRS will decide what losses, if any, you can deduct. You could end up writing a much larger check than would have been necessary had you anticipated this situation.

Some casinos will, on request, provide a computer printout of activity for slot club members. They may also furnish this to the IRS if asked or subpoenaed.

Since this record reflects only the results of play when the club card was properly inserted and applies only to the one casino, it is a finite document the IRS may view with skepticism. There is no guarantee it will provide an accurate overview of your activity.

Although I use slot club cards when I am working, I have had experiences when the card did not activate properly. I often encounter machines where the card box is out of commission or fails to register. The unit or central computer could be malfunctioning, or perhaps I was careless and failed to check that the unit acknowledged my card before I started the first spin.

I am not going to leave a machine simply because the card does not register my play. Apart from the freebie entitlements, it is immaterial to me whether or not the casino has an accurate record of my wins or losses. I keep my own record.

I have enjoyed several big wins when my club card was not functioning but I have also had losses I could have otherwise overlooked had I had not kept documentation.

My strong recommendation is, no matter what, always keep a daily activity record or similar diary for every casino visit.

Develop the habit if completing the entries for each session before you move on to the next machine. This way, if you strike a jackpot or hit a streak of small wins, you will honor the habit and bless those entries. In the meantime, the documentation will give you better control of your casino activities and considerably enhance your winning prospects.

Do not look on this as an unnecessary chore on days when you are losing. It could prove more important then. You have no input when the casino reports wins of more than $1,200 to the IRS. You do control recording your losses.

That elusive big win may not come until the last day of your final visit for the year. It will be too late then to try and resurrect what you have paid out on previous visits.

Now for the keys and padlocks I mentioned earlier.

The following keys will open the door to Winland. Use them and walk through—but don't bring along the padlocks.

Manage your luck. Throw open those Windows of Opportunity. Have fun.

Claude Halcombe's
DAILY ACTIVITY RECORD
for Slot Machine Enthusiasts

Day: 1   2   3   4
Casino: 1
Casino: 2
Date:

Session Number	Machine Number	Type of Machine	Session Investment	Session Return	Session Profit	Session Loss	Daily Balance Profit	Loss
Session 1								
Session 2								
Session 3								
Session 4								
Session 5								
Session 6								
Session 7								
Session 8								
Session 9								
Session 10								
Session 11								
Session 12								
DAILY TOTALS			$	$			$	$
Session 13								
Session 14								
Session 15								
ADJUSTED TOTALS			$	$			$	$

DAILY ACTIVITY SUMMARY

Total Sessions: Winning Sessions: Losing Sessions:
                   Biggest Win: $ Worst Loss: $
                 Smallest Win: $ Smallest Loss: $
                 Average Win: $ Average Loss: $

TOTAL INVESTMENT $ **TOTAL RETURN** $

Profit for Day: $ **Profit for Visit:** $
Loss for Day: ($)   **Loss for Visit:**   ($)

General Comments & Observations.

THE KEYS TO WINLAND

Key 1	Prepare and plan
Key 2	Set aside "free" money
Key 3	Select the right casino
Key 4	Identify the best slots to play
Key 5	Choose game plan and strategy
Key 6	Take adequate bankroll
Key 7	Expect to win
Key 8	Join the slot club
Key 9	Keep to a slot machine circuit
Key 10	Stay with the same type of machines
Key 11	Play the same denomination slots
Key 12	Play maximum coins only when appropriate
Key 13	Play your stake—not your winnings
Key 14	Stay alert at all times
Key 15	Do not seek big jackpots
Key 16	Watch other players and other machines
Key 17	Restrict number and duration of visits
Key 18	Keep appropriate records
Key 19	Update notes and strategies
Key 20	Be prepared to accept losses

THE PADLOCKS WHICH WILL KEEP YOU OUT

Padlock 1	Act on impulse, without forethought
Padlock 2	Patronize "convenience" casinos
Padlock 3	Use borrowed or committed money
Padlock 4	Arrive with an inadequate stake
Padlock 5	Bring too much money
Padlock 6	Play big denomination slots
Padlock 7	Play any slots—anywhere—anytime
Padlock 8	Expect to lose
Padlock 9	Seek big jackpots
Padlock 10	Play option-buy machines
Padlock 11	Play maximum coins at all times
Padlock 12	Take credit cards/checks with you
Padlock 13	Stay with one machine
Padlock 14	Wander aimlessly
Padlock 15	Have no game plan/no strategy
Padlock 16	Play out your winnings
Padlock 17	Drink alcohol during play
Padlock 18	Pay no attention
Padlock 19	Keep no records
Padlock 20	Chase your losses

12

Introducing the
Work Plans

Each of the following work plans shares one critically important feature with the others: When you leave a machine session, you collect your winnings and pocket them. You do not risk winnings from any session.

Even the most complicated, the Emerald Plan, is predicated upon taking your session stake plus profits out of circulation immediately and not putting them at risk again.

It differs from the other three plans inasmuch as the protocol allows you to recycle the residuals of stakes you risked on losing sessions but does not allow you to replay the stake or the winnings from any session in which you made money.

A distinction is made between credits accumulating during a session and the winnings you take away from that session.

In the Green Plan, you play the machine stake, no more no less, then take out your credits and set them aside. If the session was profitable, you take the entire stake and the winnings out of circulation; if you lost money, you put away what you have recovered of the stake.

In the Silver and Gold plans, you do likewise but both allow you to pursue hits of various levels with a specific number of two coin spins during the session.

If the hits come late, you could be putting some of the accumulated credits back into play before you cash out at the end of the session.

Nonetheless, even with these plans, you set aside every coin you have taken out, from losing and winning sessions alike, and you do not replay any of that money.

I have found the most treacherous time in any session is when I start exiting the machine with my winnings. I use the term *start* advisedly because, short of stopping dead as in the Green Plan, it is a process which can drag out, sometimes over a lot of spins, especially if you are getting small payouts as you make the move.

These small payouts can be insidious. They can eat holes into your winnings without you realizing what is happening until it's too late. Unless you have a predetermined response to them, you can find those small hits are costing you more than you are getting back each time.

The Silver, Gold, and Emerald plans have three exit strategies. Your choice is dictated by the amount and timing of hits during the exit period. At different stages during a drawn-out procedure, it is possible you will use all three.

Be careful. As these are probably the most difficult guidelines to understand and can be even more difficult to follow in actual play, be sure you familiarize yourself with all of these proven ways of leaving a machine with your winnings before you try the Silver, Gold, or Emerald plans.

My observations confirm the majority of players give back much of their winnings simply because they have no set way of leaving the machine with their profits intact. It is not easy to combat this problem. Your protection is to learn and thoroughly understand each of the exit strategies, recognize the danger of mixed signals as you get a succession of small hits, and know which signals to ignore and which to follow.

When you have played out your stake, the cardinal exit rules for all strategies except the Green Plan are:

1. Never risk more money than you got back from the last worthwhile hit as defined in the work plan.
2. Do not play more than ten spins after any worthwhile hit except in Triggers four and five for the Gold and Emerald plans, no matter how big the hit may be.

At the beginning of the description for each work plan is a summary of the various guidelines. I keep abbreviations of these summaries on cards for ready reference.

I recommend you keep an appropriate card for the work plan you intend to use on your casino visits with you at all times during your stay, especially when you are in the learning stages.

When you are working any of the three more sophisticated and difficult plans, you must be alert at all times, and be able to quickly interpret various signals and make appropriate responses.

Unless you have made a definite decision to stay with one plan during the entire visit, you should take cards for each plan with you. However, apart from the defensive fallback to the Green Plan to protect your stake when necessary, you should not switch from one plan to another during the course of a day.

Depending on my results, toward the end of a visit I do sometimes change plans from one day to the next.

The following definitions will help you understand the work plan summaries.

Target Slots: The type of slot machine for which the work plans have been devised. As all four are intended for use on two coin multipliers, inclusion of this line at the top of each summary is for reinforcement only.

Coins: Used here to indicate either dollar slugs or quarters for 25-cent machines.

Work Time: The approximate hours you will spend to complete a full day or minutes for each machine session. The two figures reflect either likely spin rates for faster players or the impact of a greater number of short losing sessions.

Machine Sessions: The number of sessions for the day. Most times this is twelve, but there is a provision to continue to fifteen sessions in the Green and Gold plans and another for replaying the balance of stakes from losing sessions in the Emerald Plan.

Daily Stake: The amount of money required to fully fund each work plan on dollar and quarter slots.

Per Session: The minimum and maximum amounts for each machine session. The letters PC indicate which plans have a provision for playing a portion of accumulated credits before exiting.

Win Goal: Each plan has a realistic goal for winning on a daily basis and for each three-day visit. This goal is expressed as percentage of the minimum stake.

Risk Factor: This is my broad assessment of the downside risks in using each plan.

Triggers: The circumstances which decide if and when you move from single coins to double coin play. Depending on the choice of plan, there can be as many as five triggers or as few as one, as in the Green Plan.

Played: The number of spins and the timing for double coin play. These vary depending on the trigger. Appropriate response is identified by the trigger number. The abbreviation **CS** is used where double coin play is for consecutive spins; **G** is for the gap between consecutive spins when the total number of spins is broken into sections.

Play Credits: Indicates which plans allow for using some accumulated credits pursuing winning hits.

Carry Over Session Stake to Next Session: Applies only to the Emerald Plan and refers to the residuals from previous losing sessions to play addtional s essions. You can choose to play any or all of the balance of the losing stakes, but you should never start any session unless you have enough stake to complete that session without touching any winnings.

Exit Plan: Indicates whether there is a fixed exit strategy or several strategies which vary depending upon hit amounts and frequencies. All but the Green Plan have variable strategies. Some examples are:

1. Exit at twenty spins if no hit of five coins or more for one coin in.
2. Exit ten spins after any payout if you do not get another hit—five coins or more for each coin in—within ten spins of the last such hit.
3. Exit if using credits, when proceeds of last payout are gone. In other words, if you have overrun your machine stake and are using credits, you do not spend more than you received from the last hit as defined in the protocol. This avoids doubling up for five or ten spins when the last hit was worth less than that.

Defense Strategy: Once you reach the sixth session, if your losses are at least 60 percent of your total stake, switch to the Green Plan—fixed stake, single coin play.

13

Work Plan One:
The Green Plan
(Capital Preservation Strategy)

SUMMARY

Target Slots: 2 Coin Multiplier, Low Top Line Jackpot

Work Time: Day: 1¾ to 2½ hrs.   Session: 9 to 12 mins.

Machine Sessions: Minimum: 12   Maximum: 15

Daily Stake: $1 Slots: $600 for 12 $750 for 15
 25¢ Slots: $180 for 12 $225 for 15

Per Session: $1 Slots: Minimum: $50   Maximum: $50
 25¢ Slots: Minimum: $15   Maximum: $15

Win Goal: Daily: +15 percent = $1 Slots: $90   25¢ Slots: $27
 Total: +10 percent = $1 Slots: $180   25¢ Slots: $54

Risk Factor: Low

Coins per Spin: One until session stake recovered

Triggers: Single hits recovering session stake
 or Cumulative credits reaching trigger point

Stake + 25%:   5 Cons. Spins   **Stake + 50%:**   10 Cons. Spins
Stake + 75%:   15 Cons. Spins   **Stake + 100%:**   20 Cons. Spins

Exit Plan: Fixed—Leave session when stake has been played

COMMENTS

This ultraconservative strategy is aimed at avoiding substantial losses rather than piling up large profits.

I recommend this work plan to beginners and those who prefer to know before they start how much time they will spend at the slots each day.

Depending on your rate of play, there will be less than 10 percent variation in elapsed time between winning and losing days. Unlike most other work plans where winning sessions take longer to complete, here they are of shorter duration since there will be fewer transactions and there is no mechanism to extend the total number of spins.

The Green Plan calls for some discipline and a little skill, has a simple protocol, and is virtually error proof.

Unless you hit a single payout, or an accumulation of smaller payouts, which exceeds your session stake, you play a single coin every spin.

When you have used all your coins, you cash out, update your daily activity record, and go to the next machine.

You play two coins only when already assured of a profit on that machine session. You never risk more than your original stake on any session and you protect your winnings because, for each spin with additional coins in play, you are reducing the total number of spins by one.

Big hits late in the session give you an advantage. For example, the protocol calls for playing additional coins for twenty consecutive spins when a hit or the accumulation of credits is twice your stake—$100 on $1 slot or 120 coins on a quarter machine.

If this trigger is reached on the tenth spin, the total number of spins will be reduced to thirty for that session; if it does not come until spin forty, total spins will be reduced only by five, to forty-five spins.

This is the only work plan where you do not pursue any win, no matter how big, beyond the limits of the stake you have allocated to each machine session.

Hit red sevens on the last spin, you take your accumulated credits and move on to the next slot just as you would have done had the spin produced nothing. The exit strategy is fixed. Play your stake and leave.

When second coins are triggered, play them consecutively for the number of times indicated in the summary or on your reference card; i.e., five times when the trigger reached is 25 percent above your stake, fifteen times if it is at the 75 percent level, and so on until your stake is exhausted.

If you are having a profitable session and hit several triggers, do not extend the sequence of additional coin spins unless each new hit recovers your stake plus the trigger profit. For example, you have seventy-five credits and have started to play the ten consecutive spins with additional coins in when you hit a payout which brings total credits beyond the 75 percent session profit mark. Take no action, continue to play out the balance of the spins you were working on.

Should the new payout bring in sixty-five coins in one hit, you either continue with the sequence you were working or switch to the new trigger, whichever offers the most spins. This is very important: Do not add the sequences together under any circumstances.

Should you deplete your stake before the end of the sequence, the session is finished.

The downside here is deliberately restricted. I have never

lost more than $240 playing the Green Plan on dollar slots; in fact, only three times have I lost $100.

I consider plus or minus 5 percent days as break-even results. In my experience with this defensive strategy, they seem to be the rule rather than the exception—which is how it should be with a defensive system. If there is any true fail-safe plan in slot machine gambling, this is about as close as it gets.

In theory, with or without a strategy, there is always a remote chance of hitting a jackpot. In terms of the number of spins, this work plan opens the Windows of Opportunity about as wide as possible, but it strictly limits exposure to two coin play in the interest of stake preservation.

You may hit a top line payout with maximum coins in but it is less likely with this strategy than with any of the others we describe. The compensation is that you have more chances of hitting one or more midsize wins and you are retaining the proceeds of all wins irrespective of size.

My biggest win with this work plan was more than $400 for the day, and I have had several in excess of $300, but most are around the target figure of plus 15 percent of my stake or less.

14

Work Plan Two:
The Silver Plan
(Moderate Loss/Gain Strategy)

SUMMARY

Target Slots: 2 Coin Multiplier, Low Top Line Jackpot

Work Time: **Day:** 1 to 2½ hours.   **Session:** 5 to 12 mins.

Machine Sessions: **Minimum:** 12   **Maximum:** 12

Daily Stake: $1 Slots: $600 for 12   25¢ Slots: $180 for 12

Per Session: **$1 Slots:** Minimum: $20   Maximum: $50 + PC
25¢ Slots: Minimum: $15   Maximum: $15 + PC

Win Goal: **Daily:** +20 percent = $1 Slots: $120   25¢ Slots: $36
Three-Day Visit: +15 percent = $1 Slots: $270   25¢ Slots: $81

Risk Factor: Low Moderate

Coins per Spin: One until payout triggers an increase

Triggers: (1) Payout recovering outlay 10 previous spins
(2) Credits exceeding session outlay at time by 10 coins but not less than 20 total
(3) Payout in excess of full session stake

Played: (1) and (2) 5 Cons. Spins   (3) 10 Cons. Spins

Play Credits: Limited to last payout proceeds or to exit

Stake Carry Over to Next Session: No

Exit Plan: Variable

(1) At 20 spins, if no hit of 5 or more coins per coin in
(2) 10 spins after any payout as defined in exit 1
(3) If using credits, when proceeds of last payout used or exit two, whichever comes first.

COMMENTS

While the downside risks in this plan are low to moderate, players should note they are significantly higher than in Work Plan One for three reasons:

1. Two coin play is triggered by payouts and credit accumulation—before there is any assurance of a profit on the full session.
2. The number of spins can be reduced by a series of smaller payouts which together do not generate a session profit.
3. A portion of session credits may be at risk.

To offset those higher risks, the chances of winning more often from controlled two coin play are improved and, should you encounter a poor session, the unused portion of your stake is taken out of play and put back into your pocket. You do not extend the number of sessions.

The Silver Plan requires a lot more attention to detail. It is hard to make a mistake using the Green Plan but here chances of error are much greater. Players must be careful and concentrate on the task at hand, especially when those small wins start coming.

The most frequent mistake is to confuse the signals which trigger two coin play, especially when there is a succession of small payouts. The protocol is to react once to each trigger and ignore any successive small hits which follow closely unless, in themselves, they generate a new trigger. For example, you have played fifteen coins and you hit or reach a credits accumulation of twenty-five coins; the protocol now calls for two coins for the next five spins and on the fourth spin, you hit for ten coins.

At this stage, you will have put in twenty-three coins and have thirty-five credits, which seems to meet the criteria in Trigger (2) [credits exceeding session outlay by ten or more coins].

This is a false trigger because you have already reacted to the twenty-five coin accumulation. All that has happened since is you have played eight more coins on four spins and have ten coins back for those plays.

Resist the impulse to start a new five spin play with two coins in. Complete the remaining, or fifth, spin in the first sequence and revert to single coin play unless you hit again and the combined total of hits triggers a new sequence based on spins played and credits registered since the previous trigger.

The rule is each trigger must stand alone. Do not react twice to the same trigger. Unless a new hit or new credits set up another trigger point, ignore them and finish the sequence you are playing.

It may sound complicated but it is not. At worst, the strategy can be a little tricky until you have learned to separate the false signals from those which call for a reaction. Provided you concentrate on the task at hand, you will quickly master the intricacies of this work plan.

This is also the first of the four strategies to tap any portion of your session credits. Within strictly defined parameters, here you may follow your winning hits beyond the limits of your session stake.

The risk to accumulated credits is small since the accent is on picking up any hits which come within 5 spins of the last hit, or a maximum of ten spins or twenty coins if that hit was large enough to recover the whole session stake.

Whether you are playing your stake or part of your credits, remember the exit rules are there to protect you.

The session is terminated if you go twenty spins either from the start or beyond a hit returning five coins or more per coin played. Smaller wins count on the meter but in no other way.

Play no more than ten spins after any payout which recovers your investment on the previous ten spins. And if you are using part of your credits, do not risk more coins than the proceeds of the last payout. This way you protect what you have won and are not suckered into extending the session because of small, inconsequential payouts.

While I have doubled my stake on occasion and made a 40 percent profit on other days, a 20 percent win expectation for the day and 15 percent for a trip are more realistic goals. My best win was more than $600 but my worst day chewed up close to $350 of my stake. However, I have had more than twice as many winning as losing days using the Silver Plan.

15

Work Plan Three:
The Gold Plan
(Elevated Risk/High Gain Strategy)

SUMMARY

Target Slots: 2 Coin Multiplier, Low Top Line Jackpot

Work Time: **Day:** 1 to 2½ hours.   **Session:** 5 to 12 mins.

Machine Sessions: **Minimum:** 12   **Maximum:** 12

Daily Stake: **$1 Slots:** $600 for 12 $750 for 15
   25¢ Slots: $180 for 12 $225 for 15

Per Session: **$1 Slots:** Minimum: $25   Maximum: $50 + PC
   25¢ Slots: Minimum: $7.50   Maximum: $15 + PC

Win Goal: **Daily:**   25% = $1 Slots: $150   25¢ Slots: $45
Three Day Visit: 20% = $1 Slots: $360   25¢ Slots: $108

Risk Factor: Moderate to High

Coins per Spin: One until payout triggers increase

Triggers: (1) Payout of five or more coins or more per coin played
   (2) Payout recovering outlay 10 previous spins
   (3) Credits exceeding session outlay at time
   (4) Single payout equivalent to session stake +

(5) Cumulative credits 200 percent of outlay at time

Played: (1) 5 cons. spins (2) and (3) 10 cons. spins
(4) 5 spins, 5 spin gap if no hit, then 10 cons. spins
(5) 5 spins, 5 spin gap if no hit, then 10 cons. spins, then
another 5 spin gap, followed by 5 cons. spins.

Play Credits: Limited to proceeds of last payout

Carry Over Session Stake to Next Session: No

Exit Plan: Variable

(1) At 20 spins if no hit of 5 coins or more for one coin in
(2) 10 spins after any payout as in exit plan one
(3) If using credits, when proceeds of last payout gone

Defense Strategy: Once you have reached the sixth session, switch to Green Plan if losses are 60 percent of the stake for sessions already completed.

COMMENTS

At first glance, there may seem little difference between this and the Silver Plan. The distinctions are subtle but do not be fooled, they are important. In fact, there is a definite acceleration in the downside risk which may or may not be offset by the chance of more big wins when everything is going well. There are no guarantees.

I have found I can lose more often with the Gold Plan than any other, and most times those losing days can chew up 40 percent, 50 percent, or even more of my daily bankroll. Despite this drawback, I seem to come through with enough solid wins to keep ahead of the game. It is not unusual for me to double my money or better using this strategy.

The danger points lie in three factors:

1. Smaller hits trigger double coin play.
2. Double coin play can be longer and staggered.
3. Sessions can be extended from twelve to fifteen

3. Sessions can be extended from twelve to fifteen machines.

Any of these can be the flash point which determines whether you will win or lose for the day; combined, they can wreak havoc on your stake or generate several big hits in one day to return a substantial profit.

The protocol follows the Silver Plan closely. In practice, the most difficult adjustment to make is to the staggered double coin plays which come with triggers four and five.

These can also be the most frustrating. The ploy is intended to leapfrog spin sequences which generally cost more to cover than they give back. The strategy sometimes backfires.

I have many times played my five double coin spins, then come back to single play, only to see double bars, three bars or sevens hit immediately.

This is disconcerting, but I have found, over a given number of days, the extra value of those hits would not have recovered the cost of playing maximum coins through those breaks. Nor have these hits come near, in value or number, the hits I enjoyed in the two coin sequences following those breaks— payouts which came beyond the point where I would have otherwise been returning to single coin play.

The consolation, when a bigger hit comes after you revert to one coin, is that since these work plans are devised for multipliers, at least you get a proportionate payout on every hit. You do not lose out altogether.

Notice the introduction of a defense strategy with this work plan. It is a part of the protocol simply because of the greater risk to your stake. I strongly recommend you take this action to protect the balance of your stake whenever the 60 percent loss threshold is breached. No matter how careful or diligent you may be with any system, there will be days when nothing seems to go right and working a system like this can produce those days from time to time.

Unlike the Silver Plan, there is a provision here to extend the number of daily sessions from twelve to fifteen but the strategy offers no built-in benchmark to automatically make that decision for you.

This is not an oversight. My results from session extensions have been so mixed I cannot offer them as valid guidelines for other players.

I will not extend sessions on any day unless the ratio of losers to winners during the twelve-session base (the Two:One theory) is so far out of whack I can logically expect to pick up two winning sessions from the three-session addition. Most times when I have done this, the winning sessions have come but, overall, the net results from the extra sessions have been a wash.

I am inclined now to end the day after session twelve no matter what, but you should make that choice yourself.

Whatever you decide, do not play fewer than twelve nor more than fifteen sessions. At one point or the other, make your decision and call it quits.

16

Work Plan Four:
The Emerald Plan
(High Risk/High Gain Strategy)

SUMMARY

Target Slots: 2 Coin Multiplier, Low Top Line Jackpot

Work Time: Day: 1 to 2½ hours.   **Session:** 5 to 12 mins.

Machine Sessions: Minimum: 12   **Maximum:** Limited by Stake

Daily Stake: **$1 Slots:** $600 for 12 $750 for 15
25¢ Slots: $180 for 12 $225 for 15

Per Session: **$1 Slots:** Minimum: $25   Maximum: $50 + PC
25¢ Slots: Minimum: $7.50 Maximum: $15 + PC

Win Goal: Daily: 25 percent = **$1 Slots:** $150   **25¢ Slots:** $45
Three-Day Visit: 20 percent = **$1 Slots:** $360   **25¢ Slots:** $108

Risk Factor: Moderate to High

Coins per Spin: One until payout triggers increase

Triggers: (1) Payout of five or more coins or more per coin played
(2) Payout recovering outlay 10 previous spins
(3) Credits exceeding session outlay at time

154

(4) Single payout equivalent to session stake +

(5) Cumulative credits 200 percent of outlay at time

Played: (1) 5 cons. spins (2) and (3) 10 cons. spins

(4) 5 spins, 5 spin gap if no hit, then 10 cons. spins

(5) 5 spins, 5 spin gap if no hit, then 10 cons. spins, then another 5 spin gap, followed by 5 cons. spins.

Play Credits: Limited to proceeds of last payout

Carry Over Session Stake to Next Session: Yes

Exit Plan: Variable

(1) At 20 spins if no hit of 5 coins or more for one coin in

(2) 10 spins after any payout as in Exit Plan one

(3) If using credits, when proceeds of last payout gone

Defense Strategy: Once you reach the sixth session, switch to Green Plan at the next Session if losses reach 60 percent of the stake for machine sessions already completed.

COMMENTS

In each of the previous work plans, part of the strategy has been to keep the results of each session separate from all other machine sessions. Whether you end the session winning or losing, you pocket all proceeds and move on. You risk neither your stake nor winnings from sessions you have already completed.

Here the emphasis changes.

After a winning machine session, the total proceeds are put out of commission, as in the other plans.

What is different here is the protocol for handling what you have left of the stakes from your losing sessions. Instead of setting these amounts aside, you recycle them into the balance of your daily program. As long as you have sufficient funds to finance additional sessions from these residual stakes and you wish to do so, you can continue.

In all other respects, the Emerald Plan is identical to the

Gold Plan but the impact of this single variation is akin to the differences between night and day. It can have a drastic effect on your results on any given day and visit.

The danger is, except for what you have taken out of circulation along with winnings from successful sessions, you continue to risk some of your stake.

Assume you are having an average day, with session losses running two to one. At the end of the twelfth regular session, you will have the residual of your stakes from eight losing sessions in the bucket or slide where you keep your stake money separate from your winnings. If you have lost 50 percent of your stake on those losing sessions, you will have enough money to bankroll at least another four sessions.

The downside here is high because that residual is again exposed to risk. In practice you could continue to play your machine stakes over and over until you lose the full amount originally allocated to those earlier sessions.

If your winning sessions showed a healthy profit, then indirectly you may be consuming those profits. You are taking the chance you will end the day with a lot less than you would using one of the other work plans.

Should your winning session profits be small or break-even, you can easily compound your total losses with this plan.

What is the upside? You have the potential to win more money more often!

Three times in twelve visits I made more than $1,000 in a day using the Emerald Plan. On one occasion my profits were more than $2,500. On most of my most profitable trips, I used this strategy at least once during the visit, generally twice.

I haven't won as frequently as I have with work plan three and some of my losing days have been worse than with any of the other systems, but there is no doubt the overall result has been more money to offset those losses.

When I plan a visit now, I do not hesitate to predicate my approach on using the Emerald Plan the first day and, depending on the outcome, again the next day or on the last day.

I have not used the Emerald Plan three days in a row because I have not won big money on two consecutive days with it and I generally play safe on the last day unless my profits for the trip are already assured.

The closest I have come to two big days during a three-day visit was more than $1,000 on the first day, a small loss with the Gold Plan the second day, and $280 profit with the Emerald Plan on the last day.

Those figures speak for themselves. I chose the Emerald Plan again for the final day on that visit because I knew I would go home a winner no matter what. As it happened, I was fortunate enough to add a little more to my profits.

A piece of advice. Do not attempt either the Gold or the Emerald Plan until you have built your skills. Both require discipline, concentration, and persistence, especially when it becomes necessary to monitor the spins during the broken sequences of double coin play.

Gambling Books Ordering Information

Ask for any of the books listed below at your bookstore. Or to order direct from the publisher, call 1-800-447-BOOK (MasterCard or Visa), or send a check or money order for the books purchased (plus $4.00 shipping and handling for the first book ordered and $1.00 for each additional book) to Carol Publishing Group, 120 Enterprise Avenue, Dept. 40584, Secaucus, NJ 07094.

Beating the Wheel: The System That's Won More Than $6 Million, From Las Vegas to Monte Carlo by Russell T. Barnhart
$14.95 paper   0-8184-0553-8   (CAN $19.95)

Beat the House: Sixteen Ways to Win at Blackjack, Craps, Roulette, Baccarat and Other Table Games by Frederick Lembeck
$12.95 paper   0-8065-1607-0   (CAN $17.95)

Blackjack Your Way to Riches by Richard Albert Canfield
$12.95 paper   0-8184-0498-1   (CAN $17.95)

The Body Language of Poker: Mike Caro's Book of Tells by Mike Caro
$18.95 paper   0-89746-100-2   (CAN $26.95)

The Cheapskate's Guide to Las Vegas: Hotels, Gambling, Food, Entertainment, and Much More by Connie Emerson
$9.95 paper   0-8065-1530-9   (CAN $13.95)

The Complete Book of Sports Betting: A New, No Nonsense Approach to Sports Betting by Jack Moore
$14.95 paper   0-8184-0579-1   (CAN $20.95)

Darwin Ortiz on Casino Gambling: The Complete Guide to Playing and Winning by Darwin Ortiz
$14.95 paper   0-8184-0525-2   (CAN $20.95)

For Winners Only: The Only Casino Gambling Guide You'll Ever Need by Peter J. Andrews
$18.95 paper   0-8065-1728-X   (CAN $26.95)

Gambling Scams: How They Work, How to Detect Them, How to Protect Yourself by Darwin Ortiz
$11.95 paper   0-8184-0529-5   (CAN $15.95)

Gambling Times Guide to Blackjack by Stanley Roberts
$12.95 paper   0-89746-015-4   (CAN $17.95)

Gambling Times Guide to Craps by N.B. Winkless
$9.95 paper   0-89746-013-8   (CAN $13.95)

How to be Treated Like a High Roller by Robert Renneisen
$8.95 paper   0-8184-0580-4   (CAN $12.95)

John Patrick's Advanced Blackjack
$19.95 paper   0-8184-0582-1   (CAN $27.95)

John Patrick's Advanced Craps
$18.95 paper   0-8184-0577-5   (CAN $26.95)

John Patrick's Blackjack
$14.95 paper   0-8184-0555-4   (CAN $19.95)

John Patrick's Craps
$16.95 paper   0-8184-0554-6   (CAN $20.95)

John Patrick's Roulette
$16.95 paper   0-8184-0587-2   (CAN $22.95)

John Patrick's Slots
$12.95 paper   0-8184-0574-0   (CAN $17.95)

Million Dollar Blackjack by Ken Uston
$18.95 paper   0-89746-068-5   (CAN $26.95)

Playing Blackjack as a Business by Lawrence Revere
$15.95 paper   0-8184-0064-1   (CAN $21.95)

Progression Blackjack: Exposing the Cardcounting Myth by Donald Dahl
$11.95 paper   0-8065-1396-9   (CAN $16.95)

Slot Smarts by Claude Halcombe
$9.95 paper   0-8184-0584-8   (CAN $13.95)

Win at Video Poker: The Guide to Beating the Poker Machines by Roger Fleming
$10.95 paper   0-8065-1605-4   (CAN $14.95)

Winning at Slot Machines by Jim Regan
$6.95 paper   0-8065-0973-2   (CAN $7.95)

Winning Blackjack in Atlantic City and Around the World by Thomas Gaffney
$7.95 paper   0-8065-1178-8   (CAN $10.95)

Winning Blackjack Without Counting Cards by David S. Popik
$9.95 paper   0-8065-0963-5   (CAN $13.95)

(Prices subject to change; books subject to availability)